Dear ~~Nathaniel Roberts~~ : Hellen

We are so very excited & happy for
you. Enjoy your new little "son"
every single second. We hope
this book adds some joy & info
during your waiting period.
Can't wait to see him!
    Much Love,

    George, Sue, Jennifer & Loren.

happy

happy

day

× × × ×

Love you. xx

baby·mAGIC

RYLAND
PETERS
& SMALL
LONDON NEW YORK

Teresa Moorey

baby MAGIC

Enchanting ideas and traditional
wisdom for you and your baby

First published in the USA in 2004
by Ryland Peters & Small, Inc.
519 Broadway, 5th Floor
New York, NY 10012
www.rylandpeters.com

10 9 8 7 6 5 4 3 2 1

Library of Congress Cataloging-in-
Publication Data

Moorey, Teresa.
  Baby magic : enchanting ideas and
traditional wisdom for you and your baby /
Teresa Moorey.
    p. cm.
  Includes index.
  ISBN 1-84172-693-1
  1. Magic. 2. Infants--Miscellanea. I. Title.
  BF1611.M66 2004
  133.4'3'0832--dc22
                          2004009288

Printed and bound in China.

Senior designer Catherine Griffin
Editor Sharon Ashman
Picture research Claire Hector
Production Deborah Wehner
Art director Gabriella Le Grazie
Publishing director Alison Starling

Editorial consultant Christina Rodenbeck
Index Diana Le Core

Note
Neither the author nor the publisher can be
held responsible for any claim arising out of
the use or misuse of suggestions made in
this book. While every effort has been made
to ensure that the information contained in
the book is accurate and up to date, it is
advisory only and should not be used as an
alternative to seeking specialist medical advice.

CONTENTS

mAGiCAL baby

Do you believe in magic? If you have ever touched a snowflake, smelled a hyacinth, or seen a tiny chick peck its way out of an egg, then you cannot doubt it. Once you have held your own child in your arms, you will be totally convinced.

This enchantment is more than a feeling—it is a force. Just by becoming a parent, your perspectives will widen and your priorities will alter. If you have never before been aware of this power, it may now be obvious to you. This book is about tuning in to the magic that is all around you, letting it enrich your life and empower your visions and desires. In this your baby will be your companion—and possibly your teacher.

It is amazing how several things in an ordinary toy box have magical and traditional associations, and I shall show you how you can kit out your baby and yourself for conjuring. But, to begin with, a little magic certainly goes a long way when you are trying to get pregnant, as your body is naturally sharply attuned to what goes on in your mind. For this there is a fertility spell for you to try. Later, when you know that an amazing new life is growing within you, you will want to feel bonded with it, even to communicate. This you can do only by entering her or his Dreamtime world by means of a magical meditation. Once the new arrival is here, something extra special is needed to welcome baby to his or her new world. As you get to know your child in a thousand unforgettable ways, you will want to explore, experience, and maximize the wonderment of it all. Giving your child a name is in itself a magical act because a name is a vibration that he or she will carry all through life. With the help of this book you can tune in to the name your child wants and conduct a special naming ceremony that recognizes the importance of this. Protecting your child and fostering loving bonds with other relatives will also be of paramount importance and will benefit from a little occult oomph!

As time passes, being with your baby will open you to the beauty of life and the promise of the future in a way you never imagined. You can celebrate the seasons and the cycles of Nature in the knowledge that these are fresh and amazing to your baby. And when the single candle is lit on that first birthday cake, you will understand its hidden meanings and secretly celebrate your own year of enchantment.

Now you will always have a touch of magic to keep you alive to the true meanings of existence, and to give yourself and your baby the very, very best—of all worlds.

"When I dipt into the future, far as human eye could see,
Saw the Vision of the world, and all the wonder that would be."

LOCKSLEY HALL, ALFRED, LORD TENNYSON (1809–1892)

mAGicAL

TOY BOX

the MAGIC of babies

From the top of his downy head to the tips of his toes, a baby is perfection. Newly arrived in this world, he is still only a hair's breadth from Otherworld—the world of Spirit. Often, when you look into your baby's eyes, you may feel you are gazing at a creature who, although pure and innocent, is unfathomably wise. This may be because your baby has lived many lives before and still recalls some of those past incarnations.

As your baby's eyes start to focus, you may find that they seem to follow the movements of things you cannot see. This may well be because your baby truly can see Spirits. As children grow, they learn not to perceive certain things as they become conditioned by the expectations of the adults around them. No such conditioning has, as yet, obscured your baby's clear sight. Try to follow his vision and open out to the subtle realms.

As far as your baby is concerned, anything is possible and everything is wonderful. Each moment is an adventure, a voyage of discovery. Let your baby help you to reconnect with your own lost perceptions. Hold your baby when he is asleep and do the following simple spell to retrace your steps into your past, to a time when your eyes also were clear and bright enough to see beyond the veil.

"Every baby born into the world is a finer one than the last"

NICHOLAS NICKLEBY, CHARLES DICKENS (1812–1870)

CONNECTING TO YOUR CHILDHOOD

This exercise can be repeated as often as you like to connect you to the insights and clear vision of childhood. Soon you, too, will see Spirits.

YOU WILL NEED:

A purple candle

An amethyst geode or piece of amethyst, as large as you can find

Sandalwood oil, or a pleasant fragrance familiar to you as a small child, such as lavender or roses

An oil burner

A photograph of yourself as a child (optional)

A notebook

You will need to collect all the items needed and put them close by, at a time when you know your little one will be drowsy. Light the candle and try to make sure that the flame is reflected in the amethyst. Heat the oil in the burner. Breathe in the fragrance deeply. Look at your sleeping baby and let yourself tune in to how it feels to be so small and for the world to be so fresh.

Fix your mind on a happy time from as early as possible in your childhood. Look for a while at your photograph, if you have one. Then look deep into the amethyst and let your mind drift. Really be that small child again. Go back in time and reconnect with how it felt and how the world appeared to your childish eyes. Do this for as long as you like—you may find your awareness drifts in and out or that you go into a long reverie.

When you are ready to finish, put out the candle and the oil burner. Make a note of all the things you have felt in a special magical notebook. Have a cup of tea or juice, to bring you properly back to the here and now.

MAGICAL toy box

As you become open to the magic of life, so you become aware that everything has a subtle essence, a meaning beyond ordinary function and appearance. Some things are more obvious in this respect than others. For instance, a red rose is more than just a sweet-smelling, pretty flower—it spells love. A dove is more than a bird—it means peace. To a greater or lesser extent, all things have a meaning, and living magically means being aware of this.

To do magic with and for your baby, you will need a collection of objects that have special symbolic significance. Many of these will be specific to the spell or ritual in question, but there are some things that you will use repeatedly. Enjoy collecting them and keep them in a special closet or box so they retain their aura of enchantment.

☆ YOUR TOY BOX ☆

These items should make up your basic box of magical tools as they will be used repeatedly throughout the spells in this book.

A CHRISTENING MUG • this is a baby version of a chalice. It can be used to symbolize the element of Water
A CHALICE OR SPECIAL WINE GLASS • for you to drink from
A LARGE FLAT STONE • this symbolizes the element of Earth
NOTEBOOK • to record various spells, activities, or poignant moments
MOON PHASE CALENDAR • to tell you the phases of the moon
SOFT TOYS • a variety to represent the four elements (see page 13)
A WAND • you can use a child's toy one if you like, or find your own outdoors—a branch is ideal
A RATTLE • use baby's. A rattle can wake up the area you use for your spell
A BELL • use it in the same way as a rattle

CANDLES • you will need a supply of these. White can be used for any purpose, but it is nice to have a selection of colors for different spells. Candles may be used to symbolize the element of Fire
ESSENTIAL OIL AND BURNER • it is a good idea to have a selection, such as lavender, jasmine, orange, sandalwood, patchouli, frankincense, eucalyptus, cinnamon, and bergamot, as they keep well if stored in the dark
A SELECTION OF CRYSTALS • rose quartz, amethyst, clear crystal, for example, as specified in the spells
JOSS STICKS AND HOLDER • lavender, cinnamon, frankincense, patchouli, jasmine—joss sticks may symbolize the element of Air

THE MAGIC CIRCLE

Occultists perform their rites inside a magic circle, which is created by the mind and strengthened by ritual. The circle helps to contain the spell until you are ready to release it. It also acts as protection. It is a good idea to form your circle for spells, but always remember to release the spell from it and to banish the circle when it's no longer needed.

YOU WILL NEED:

A wand

Salt

A small glass of water

A selection of soft toys

You can make your circle simply by visualizing a circle or sphere of light around you. Even better "draw" it in the air clockwise (counterclockwise in the Southern Hemisphere) using your wand or fingertip, starting in the north (south in the Southern Hemisphere). Cleanse your circle by blowing away negativity and sprinkling salt and water inside it.

Ask the elemental guardians to be present, Earth in the north, Air in the east, Fire in the south, and Water in the west. (Reverse Fire and Earth in the Southern Hemisphere). Soft toys are a colorful way of representing the elements for baby spells. Use a brown teddy for Earth, a yellow or blue bird for Air, a lion for Fire, and a dolphin for Water. Earth will keep you safe and grounded, Air will free your mind, Fire will inspire you, and Water will soothe and heal. Keep this group of toys ready in the nursery to provide balance and protection for your baby.

Forming your circle is a spell in itself, and you may want to place yourself and baby inside one at certain times for peace, protection, or to intensify whatever meditation or ritual you are performing.

trailing CLOUDS of GLORY ...

The majority of people believe in some form of Afterlife. Advances in science are discovering the probability of other dimensions, coming closer and closer to a proof that there are worlds other than our own. But if there is an Afterlife, then why not also a Beforelife? Does it not seem likely that your baby's spirit existed before his body? If you believe this may be the case, how best might you maintain that spiritual connection while still enabling your babe to engage firmly with this material plane? Or if you believe that your babe is new in every way, but are still aware of spiritual realms, what is the safest way to make contact?

By your love, closeness, contact with your body, and all the reassurance you give, you are affirming your babe's connection with the here and now. In a way that is the easy part. When it comes to maintaining benevolent contact with the subtle realms, the best thing to do is to ask.

Every time you send out a sincere request for spiritual guidance, it is heard in the ether. Tradition holds that every child has a Guardian Angel—in fact, the 18th-century mystic Emanuel Swedenborg stated that we all have two. If you do not find the Judaeo-Christian idea of angels appealing, think of it as a Guardian Spirit. Either way, you can be sure that your babe is being watched over and cared for by eyes that see farther than your own.

"Our birth is but a sleep and a forgetting:
The Soul that rises with us, our life's Star,
Hath had elsewhere its setting,
And cometh from afar"

ODE ON INTIMATIONS OF IMMORTALITY, WILLIAM WORDSWORTH (1770–1850)

ANGELS FOR YOUR BABE

Angels are probably beings of a higher order than us, some of whom choose to help humans. They are neither masculine nor feminine. Angels are often pictured as having wings and long robes, but such perceptions are colored by our culture. Angels are said to leave a feather to show they have been close. Look out for a feather near your child's crib. Make a small gift to charity to show you appreciate the Spirit's help. You may ask for the help of one of the four major archangels to help you connect with your babe's own by lighting a candle of the appropriate color, having the angel's symbol close by, and by burning the oil special to that angel.

MICHAEL • archangel of light and warrior angel. In Jewish tradition he battles continually with darkness. He carries scales, and the cherubim were created from his tears. His color is gold, his oil orange or frankincense, and citrine or crystal quartz is his stone.

GABRIEL • means "strength of God." He speaks in dreams and bestows psychic gifts and fertility. He is the angel of the Moon, and it was he who parted the Red Sea waters to allow the Hebrews to escape from Egypt. To Muslims he is the Spirit of Truth who gave the Koran to Mohammed. His symbol is the lily or scepter, his color silver, his stone the moonstone or fire opal, and his oil is jasmine or mimosa.

RAPHAEL • is the healing archangel and a guide to those who travel. He especially guards the young. His healing wings are spread over the earth and all her creatures, and the waters of the Deep. He carries a pilgrim's staff, a wallet, and a fish, offering support and nourishment. His color is green, his stone is aquamarine or jade, and his oil is myrrh or pine.

URIEL • his name means "fire of God" and, while he brings salvation, he is associated with the power of earthquakes and volcanoes. Another version of the name, Auriel, means "light of God." To Hebrew mystics he taught the secrets of the Kabbalah. He is an angel of courage. His color is red, his stone amber or carnelian, and his oil is sandalwood or rosemary.

discover your PROTECTIVE SYMBOL

When you are pregnant, you may feel very vulnerable. This is not just because you are aware that physically you are not as able as you were, or even because you want to protect your precious bump. You may also have an increased perception of the world as a scary place to be, your mind may be full of "what ifs" or you may simply feel "wobbly." Possibly you have fears about the birth and your baby's welfare. All these feelings are perfectly natural. It is a good idea to talk about them to your health practitioner or other moms. However, deep inside you will feel better if you do the visualization spell on page 17 to find your protective symbol.

In pregnancy, especially in the first three and the last three months, you will probably find it very easy to get into a dreamy and relaxed state. When in that state you can take a "journey" inside your mind, a kind of waking dream with a purpose. The purpose here is to find your personal, protective symbol. Once you know this symbol, you can recall it whenever you need it. Although completely abstract, this symbol is very powerful because it can change your state of mind and so the world around changes with you. But more than that, it's a bit of magic!

☆ **PROTECTIVE PLANTS** ☆
- *Grow violets in your home and carry a flower with you*
- *Keep mint growing on your windowsill and wear a sprig under your watch strap to keep you healthy*
- *Train some ivy over your doorway*
- *Burn a cinnamon-scented joss stick*

FINDING YOUR PROTECTIVE SYMBOL

Settle yourself by candlelight (a white or lilac candle is best). Burn jasmine or lavender oil and follow this visualization. Record it on a cassette, if you like.

YOU WILL NEED:

A white or lilac candle

Jasmine or lavender oil

An oil burner

You are in a theater and before you there is a curtained stage. Watch as the curtains open, showing you a wide, sandy plain. Ahead there is an oasis and beyond this stands a pyramid. Go up onto the stage and walk towards the pyramid. [*Pause to visualize*]

Your feet are on a smooth path now, although on all sides the golden sands stretch, undulating, to the horizon. You are walking toward the pyramid and it looms larger and larger. [*Pause to visualize*]

Now you are walking through the oasis. The palm trees shade you, and on either side of you lie clear and peaceful pools of water. You are coming closer and closer to the pyramid and you are becoming aware of the scent of incense. [*Pause to visualize*]

Now you enter through the shadowed door of the pyramid. Your eyes take a while to become acclimatized to the soft light. You see ahead of you an altar draped in a deep red cloth. On it stands a censer and a jeweled casket with two candles burning on either side of it. There may be other articles or figures personal to you. [*Pause to visualize*]

Approach the altar slowly and reverently. When you are there, open the jeweled casket. Inside it is your personal, protective symbol. Take this out and keep it with you. Sprinkle some more incense into the censer as an offering. Give thanks in your own way. [*Pause to visualize*]

Walk backwards out of the pyramid, turn and walk back the way you came, keeping your symbol with you. When you get back to your theater, descend from the stage and place your symbol somewhere safe in the auditorium. Come back to everyday awareness when you are ready.

After your visualization, make careful note of your symbol and any other experiences you had—do not try to rationalize them. You could do a sketch, if you like. Tap yourself lightly all over and have a drink of water. Depending on the nature of your symbol, you may like to find an actual representation of it. You now have protection in the spirit realms—there is none more powerful.

ANTICIPATING

A hAPPy EVENT

NATURAL fertility

When you are trying to become pregnant, there is no harm in giving Nature a little helping hand. Fertility spells are some of the easiest to work because your own body is involved. When your spells take their effect on your unconscious, your body instinctively responds.

It is amazing how many people, having been told by doctors that they were destined never to have a child, have nonetheless been successful in conceiving, and have gone on to have a healthy baby, and in many cases more than one.

There is a mystery surrounding the whole process of pregnancy and birth, but the more relaxed you are and the more positive your frame of mind, the better a position you will be in to allow new life to flow in and join yours when trying to conceive. Meditate each day, if you can. Imagine yourself holding your baby happily and confidently. Enjoy life as much as possible, and smile! Nature is wonderful.

☆ FOLK FERTILITY ☆

Much folk wisdom exists regarding plants and fertility. Here is a small selection you can try.

- *In Hawaii and Tahiti eating bananas confers fertility—but break them from the bunch instead of cutting them*
- *Brahmins carried rice to ward off evil, but rice is also a fertility symbol and you may carry a little in your pocket or bag for that purpose*
- *In ancient Rome pictures of grapes were painted in gardens to make them fertile. Why not find some ornaments, prints, or a frieze on a grape theme to display in your bedroom?*
- *Greek brides wore a crown of olive leaves to ensure fertility—as a substitute, carry an olive stone*
- *Put a daffodil in your bedroom*
- *Eat carrot seeds, fresh figs, or sunflower seeds*
- *Carry any type of nut*
- *Burn oil or incense of patchouli*

A HELPING HAND

Before doing your spell, make sure that you get out into the elements as much as possible. Give this a full month if you can, experiencing sun, wind, and rain, the cycle of the Moon, touching trees, and if possible, doing a little gardening, sowing seeds, repotting houseplants, and so on. Also, eat healthily and avoid alcohol and nicotine.

YOU WILL NEED:

Lilies – preferably growing in a pot, but stems in water will do, as will a flowering peace lily

A white feather

An egg-shaped container such as people use to hold Easter gifts (if this is difficult to find, make your own small "egg" by cutting and gluing an egg box and painting it green)

Jasmine oil or jasmine-scented joss stick

Two white candles

A pomegranate seed, acorn, or peach stone

When the Moon is waxing, put the lilies on a windowsill in the sunlight. On three consecutive mornings and evenings, gently stroke off a little lily pollen with the feather, catching it carefully in your opened egg container. It doesn't matter if the amount you stroke off is microscopic or if you spill some, but be careful because lily pollen will stain, so avoid getting it on your clothes. After each time you collect some pollen, put the top back on the egg and store it under your bed.

At the end of the three days, perform the rest of your spell. If there is no lily scent, burn your jasmine oil or joss stick and light your candles. Place your opened egg between them. Now concentrate on your belly. Feel warmth and new life glowing there. Imagine the light from the two candles streaming within you, uniting and forming into a shining baby. Spend as long as you want imagining your baby growing inside you and you holding your baby.

Put your peach stone, acorn, or pomegranate seeds into the egg along with the pollen, and replace the cover. Keep this under your bed until you conceive. Relight the candles when you make love, or whenever you wish.

NURSERY NOTIONS

Preparing the space for your coming child is a joy. Treasure this opportunity, because after babe has arrived you won't have the time for organizing and decorating—at least not for a while.

The Chinese system of Feng Shui teaches that the space we inhabit has a subtle effect on us and many symbolic meanings. This is a complex study, but there are two simple principles you can apply to your baby's space.

The Chinese believe that the life force "chi" flows within and around everything. First, stand at the door of the nursery and ask yourself, if you were the "chi," where would you flow too fast (these are areas where there are too many straight lines or openings in line with each other, such as windows and doors)? And where might you go stagnant? Identify any dark corners or spaces behind chairs. Move furniture if you can and position wind chimes, plants, mirrors, and pictures where they can soften or enliven the chi, as necessary.

Second, if you are intending to have a chair for nursing your baby, position it in the "Honored Guest" place; this is with your back to the wall, facing the door. This position will make you feel more secure and relaxed when nursing.

If you don't have a separate room for a nursery, then these principles can be applied elsewhere.

"Sweet babe, in thy face
Soft desires I can trace,
Secret joys and secret smiles,
Little pretty infant wiles"
A CRADLE SONG, WILLIAM BLAKE (1757–1827)

Faerie mural

Murals are a fantastic way to increase depth within the room and to add enchantment. If you aren't up to doing one yourself, ask an artistic friend to help. Take a peek ahead to pages 54–77 where you will find the four elements described. Each of these is associated with a magical faerie city—a place in Otherworld where wise creatures of another dimension have their dwelling. Depicting all of them will give your child balance, protection, and inspiration.

Gorias is the city of Air, cloud-girdled towers with flying white pennants, swooping birds, dizzy cliffs, and cascading waterfalls. Finias is the city of Fire, buildings of huge stone blocks with strange inscriptions lying on desert sands, shaded by eucalyptus and date palms. Murias is the city of Water, a mighty cathedral surrounded by glistening roofs and spanned by a turquoise sea, while trees in various hues of autumn adorn the hills behind. Falias is the city of Earth, metal towers topped by enormous, glittering crystals—a faerie metropolis of parks, temples, wide roads, bridges, and a multitude of buildings all shining with a subtle glow. The traditional links are north for Earth, east for Air, south for Fire, and west for Water (with Fire and Earth reversed in the Southern Hemisphere)—stick with these if you can and let your imagination have full rein.

☆ NURSERY COLORS ☆

If you're not quite sure what color to choose for the nursery, this list may inspire you.

WHITE • *this is clean and crisp, a great background for showing off pictures and ornaments. However, too much white has rather a cold and exposed feel*
BLUE • *a soft blue is very peaceful and uplifting, but rather cool. This color works well in a room which receives lots of sun*
GREEN • *this is therapeutic. It also gives an impression of the bounty of Nature. Avoid sharp limes or muddy hues*
PINK • *an affectionate color that will make you and babe feel snuggly. It could make you more emotional however, and you may not want it for a boy*
PEACH • *orange hues make you and babe feel happier. Peach is a compromise on pink for a little boy. Be careful not to choose a color that is too strong or babe will want to play all night*
LILAC • *very peaceful, great for sweet dreams—not so good for waking up!*
YELLOW • *a mentally stimulating color, yellow will encourage babe's creativity. Avoid citrus or muddy shades*
STRONG PRIMARY COLORS • *it is tempting to decorate the nursery in bright colors, like a toy box. For some babies this works well, but others find it too stimulating for sleep*

ENCHANTED layette

As you dream about holding your new baby in your arms, collecting the layette is a sweet pleasure. All the soft fabrics and tiny clothes are irresistible, and you may want to spend time washing, folding, and storing them. Try to be relaxed while you are doing this, pouring as much love as you can into everything so baby will be wrapped in it.

Buying your layette is wonderful retail therapy. Be careful, however, of spending on things you don't really need. Take the advice of friends who already have a child regarding what is essential and what isn't.

Don't be afraid to get some things secondhand. Of course you will want everything fresh and special for your babe. However, some articles get so little use that it is unnecessary to buy new when serviceable secondhand items are available. It is fine to buy a used crib (although it is advisable to buy a new mattress) and highchair, for example, just make sure no parts are protruding that could harm your baby. However, car seats and safety equipment should always be bought new, so you can be sure they are undamaged and meet current safety requirements.

BLESSING THE LAYETTE

Give your layette a blessing with this simple spell. It will make your layette extra special and enhance your fulfillment.

YOU WILL NEED:

A crystal

Some sunshine

Your new baby items

Cleanse your crystal beforehand using the cleansing spell, below, if you like. Hang the crystal in the window where it will catch the rays of the sun and break into tiny rainbows. Make sure that one of the rainbows falls on your layette items. Imagine smiles, fun, wonderful discoveries, and happy events. Say,

> "Bright rainbow, dance into our lives
> Bless my child and make him thrive."

Leave the crystal in the window—you can use it over and over again for different items, and baby will be fascinated by the multicolored lights.

CLEANSING USED ITEMS

Naturally you will want to clean everything that has been previously used with extra-special care. But items need a psychic cleansing, too.

YOU WILL NEED:

An organic lemon

Spring water

A white cloth

A frankincense-scented joss stick

Do this spell when the moon is waning, if possible. Cut the lemon in half and squeeze the juice out. Pour it into the spring water. Dip the white cloth into the lemon solution and carefully wipe over the object to be cleansed. As you do so, imagine all the old influences being cleansed away and magically dissolved by the lemon juice. (You do not have to be too thorough over this—it is symbolic. You will already have removed the "ordinary" dirt). Say,

> "Lemon fresh, lemon clean
> Wipe away all dirt unseen."

When you feel ready, light the joss stick and pass it over and around the object so that the smoke embraces it. You can now feel confident that the item is pure for your baby.

This spell can be used for the entire nursery—just wipe some solution around the baseboards, doorway, and windowsill.

magical BABY SHOWER

When it comes to getting the most out of your baby
shower, magic is your essential helper. People love to
give and to feel part of the forthcoming happy event.
After all, by having a baby you too are making a gift—
to the process of life. Of course, your baby shower
isn't just about what you can get materially, it's a
celebration in advance of the new little infant. Conjure the right atmosphere and your
unborn child will be caught in a shower of gold.

The spell opposite has a star theme, not just because your babe will be a "little star,"
but because the five-point star is an important magical symbol relating to the Goddess.
Not only does it look like a female figure (the six-point star suggesting more of a male
shape), but it also suggests the four elements (see pages 60–67) with the human mind
as the fifth apex. Not that this needs spelling out. As with many magical matters, this is
instinctive—stars will create sparkle!

☆ **PLANTS ASSOCIATED WITH RICHES** ☆
*Where appropriate, the following plants and fruit could be
served at your baby shower or used to decorate the room.
Also, you could choose china that features them.*

Allspice	*Cinnamon*	*Mint*	*Pomegranate*
Blackberry	*Clover*	*Nutmeg*	*Stalks of wheat*
Camellia	*Ginger*	*Oak leaves*	
Cedar	*Honeysuckle*	*or acorns*	
Chamomile	*Maple*	*Pineapple*	

☆ **HINTS FOR A MAGICAL BABY SHOWER** ☆
- *Have a leisurely lavender-scented bath beforehand—if you are
relaxed, then your guests will be*
- *Keep all catering very simple—your guests have come to see you,
not to sample your cuisine*
- *Enjoy being the center of attention*
- *Wear a small star on a pendant or earrings*
- *Have a baby shower book in which guests write a wish for your
baby (with a star on the cover, if possible)*
- *Send thank-you cards—showing stars, if possible*

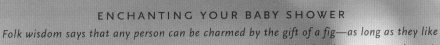

ENCHANTING YOUR BABY SHOWER

Folk wisdom says that any person can be charmed by the gift of a fig—as long as they like them, that is. The fig is also a symbol of fertility and is ruled by the planet Jupiter, champion of prosperity and generosity.

YOU WILL NEED:

Stars made from ready-to-roll icing or decorating icing that comes in a squeezy tube—gold is a good color choice

Little fig cookies

Put the stars on each fig cookie. If your guests are on a diet, try cutting apples crosswise to expose the little star at the center and sprinkle them with lemon juice to prevent them from turning brown, and a little Jupiter-ruled clove. You could add almonds, grapes, orange segments, or pecans as a garnish, since they all attract treasure. Make sure you extend the star theme into mugs, plates, and napkins and sprinkle a tray to bring in the drinks with star table confetti.

Before your guests arrive, enchant your fig cookies or pieces of fruit by placing them in front of you, holding one hand out toward them palm downward and the other on your rounded belly. Imagine the rolls connecting your baby to treasure, love, and warmth. Imagine your guests feeling happy, heartened, and generous. Light a star-shaped candle, sit back, and get ready to shine!

mysterious NEWCOMER

Your baby is growing inside you, under your heart—so near, yet so far. You may find you often try to picture her face, how she will behave, just what sort of a new human being is coming into the world to be part of your life. All your emotions are conveyed to your baby through the beating of your heart, your movements, the flow of hormones. Could it be that you can also sense the way she is feeling? Try this meditation to get in contact with the spirit of your babe, and in the peace you engender, you may find there is much about her you just "know."

Pregnancy meditation

You may record this on a cassette if you like so you can play it back when you are ready. Put some jasmine oil in your burner and relax as deeply as you can. Follow this visualization.

You are walking along a moonlit beach. The sand is soft and smooth, and the moonlight pearls the surface of the water. You can smell the fresh fragrance of the still, warm air. You can hear the slow, rhythmic swell of the waves. Take your time to absorb all the peace and beauty of your surroundings. [*Pause to visualize*]

Ahead you see a boat. Walk toward it and get in. The boat is full of soft pillows. Recline and make yourself comfortable. This vessel is safe and strong. Are you willing to take a journey on it? If so, feel the boat begin to drift gently out to sea. Feel it rocking on the waves, hear the water lapping its sides, and taste the salt on your tongue. [*Pause*]

Now the boat has drifted into a cave. The moonlight has gone and all around you there is darkness. You smell the sweet, mysterious scent of the earth. The lapping of the waves now sounds remote and muffled. You look deep into the darkness and see a pinprick of light, growing. As the light expands, you see that there is a being within it. This being is the spirit of your unborn child. [*Pause to visualize*]

Take the time to commune with this spirit. Do not jump to conclusions, for some impressions may be symbolic. Allow yourself to be absorbed in this for as long as feels comfortable. [*Pause*]

Now the light is fading and the spirit departs for the present. You say your farewells, and the boat begins to drift out of the cave. Once more you are surrounded by moonlight as the vessel bears you back to the seashore. You get out and feel your feet firm upon the sand.

Come back to everyday awareness and write down your experience. Drink some juice or water to bring you back to the here and now.

A NAME FOR YOUR CHILD

During or soon after doing the meditation you may have a strong impression of the name your child would like to have in this life. All names have meanings, and you may like to bear these in mind. Here is a selection of some of the most popular.

ADAM • Hebrew "formed of the red earth"

ALEXANDER • Greek "man who defends"

BENJAMIN • Hebrew "son of my right hand"

CHRISTOPHER • Greek "Christ's bearer"

DANIEL • Hebrew "God is my judge"

DAVID • Hebrew "beloved"

HENRY • Teutonic "ruler"

JACOB • Hebrew "one who supplants"

JONATHAN • Hebrew "God's gift"

JOSEPH • Hebrew "he shall aid"

LUKE • Latin "light"

MATTHEW • Latin "gift of God"

OLIVER • Teutonic "kind"

SAMUEL • Hebrew "of God"

WILLIAM • Teutonic "strong protector"

ABBIE (ABIGAIL) • Hebrew "joy of my father"

BECKY (REBECCA) • Hebrew "one who is bound"

CHARLOTTE • French "little woman"

CHLOE • Greek "young"

DIANA • Hebrew "Goddess"

ELIZABETH • Hebrew "God's oath"

EMILY • Latin "winning"

HANNAH • Hebrew "graceful"

ISABEL • Spanish "God's consecrated"

JESSICA • Hebrew "one who is wealthy"

KATE (KATHERINE) • Greek "pure"

LUCY • Latin "light"

MEGAN • Gaelic "pearl"

NATASHA • Russian, from Latin "birthday"

ZOE • Greek "life"

GODDESS watches over you

When you become a mother, you are arguably doing the most valuable job there is, because you are creating the generations of the future. The way you bring up your child will echo down the ages, as your influence is passed on.

To help and support you in your role, there are a number of manifestations of the Goddess that you may choose to honor. Your Goddess will understand you as no male God can, because She has been there, She knows all about your hopes and fears. Choose a Goddess to look over you from the list on the page opposite or do some further research. Find out all you can about the "story" of your Goddess. Honor your chosen Goddess by setting aside a shelf as a shrine—and get yourself a friend in high places.

GODDESS IN YOUR SHRINE

On your special shelf you can place a statue or picture of your Goddess, symbols or animals associated with her, candles, an oil burner, joss sticks or incense, a chalice, gems, stones, a moon calendar, a plant, a vase of flowers, seasonal greenery, fruits, and so on. Go with what you feel. Burn candles and incense to honor her and bring your prayers to her.

ISIS • a very complete form of the Goddess from ancient Egypt. She is great for single moms as she raised the infant Horus alone after her husband Osiris was killed. Tender, nurturing, yet feisty and powerful, she gave the pharaohs their right to rule. Her symbols include ruby, sapphire, lily, geranium, eagle, snake, myrrh, wand, scepter, throne.

KUAN YIN • healing, gentle Goddess from Buddhist China, she sacrificed her heavenly bliss to help humans. Her image is found in most Chinese homes—jade, lotus, lion, suckling infant.

DEMETER • Greek and Roman Earth Mother. Her daughter Persephone was abducted by Pluto, god of the Underworld. She returns to her mother for the summer months, but goes below ground in winter, when her mother mourns. Her symbols are pearl, cat's eye, cypress, sunflower, lion, myrrh, ear of wheat.

GAIA • primordial Greek Earth Mother who created all. Choose from holey stone, amber, all fruits and flowers

LAKSHMI • beautiful Hindu Goddess of good fortune and abundance, born from the sea, wife of Vishnu, and mother of Kama, the God of love. Rock crystal, willow, ivy, sphinx, and cardamom are her symbols.

FREYA • beloved, voluptuous Teutonic goddess, protector of marriages and queen of the Valkyries. Choose from pearl, emerald, rose, cypress, lynx, dove, and sandalwood.

YEMAYA • Nigerian and Brazilian "Fish Mother." Brazilian slaves made her their supreme Goddess. She gave birth to Sun and Moon, and two streams came from her breasts to form a lake. Every New Year's Eve thousands of people bring gifts to her on Copacabana beach, including pearl, coconut, lotus, fish, and crab.

SEHU • Cherokee maize Goddess, wife of the hunter god Kanati. She is seen as an old woman, and the corn, as giver of life, is her reborn. Malachite, emerald, magnolia, and corn on the cob are her symbols.

BRIDE • Celtic Goddess of creativity, fertility, and inspiration, an independent Goddess, great for single moms (also known as Bridget). Choose any work of craftsmanship or poetry, sacred flame (candle in a glass holder), white chalcedony, moonstone, wolf, snake, lemon balm, sandalwood, or jasmine.

great EXPECTATIONS

The months when you are pregnant are among the most special of your life. Just by sitting quietly, you are accomplishing a miracle as, deep within you, new life is growing. This is a time to treasure, but it may also be a time of anxiety because we all fear the unknown. You have been swept up in the tide of Creation, and the future is always a mystery. Mother Nature, however, realizes that you are about her business and has plenty of helpful gifts up her ample sleeve!

Don't hesitate to be open with yourself about your feelings, because only in this way can you find out what help you need and how to get it. Talking to a friend can sometimes help clarify your emotions. Rest assured that whatever the problem, there is always help available. The following rituals will help you to tap into your most important element—your subconscious mind. Along with the ancient association of the ingredients, you have some powerful tools at your service.

"It is a beauteous evening, calm and free
The holy time is quiet as a Nun
Breathless with adoration"
MISCELLANEOUS SONNETS, WILLIAM WORDSWORTH (1770–1850)

SOOTHING FRAYED NERVES

You may need some help to relax when you are pregnant. When you are feeling tired, stressed, or need help sleeping, try this calming spell.

YOU WILL NEED:

Lavender oil

An oil burner

Lavender is an all-purpose oil of which the contra-indications are almost nil. You can also use it neat upon the skin. Heat some lavender oil in a burner and as the vapors rise, imagine that a soft lilac mist is growing around you. Anoint yourself with a drop of oil on your belly saying, "Little one, rest safely"; between your breasts saying, "Heart, be at peace"; and a drop on your forehead between your eyes saying, "Mind, be free to dream."

Wipe off any excess oil with cotton pads and put the cotton wool beneath your pillow. Sleep soundly!

COURAGE BOOSTER

Anticipating the birth and what lies beyond can be scary. Women have felt like this since time began, but remember that the Goddess looks after the carriers of new life.

YOU WILL NEED:

Yellow food coloring

A glass of water

A drinking straw

A red candle

A piece of carnelian

A small red drawstring bag

Put enough drops of food coloring in the water to turn it yellow. Put the straw in the water and blow bubbles through it. As you do this, imagine all your fears going down into the water and dissolving. Imagine this for as long as you can and continue blowing a little after you have stopped imagining. Put the glass out of your sight. Light the red candle and hold the carnelian out toward it. Imagine energy, strength, and courage going into the carnelian in a stream of light. Put the carnelian in the drawstring bag and keep it with you wherever you go and close to you when giving birth. Throw the yellow water away outside, onto the earth.

TEA FOR A LATE BABY

Raspberry is ruled by Venus and signifies protection and love. Raspberry leaf tea is traditionally taken to hasten the arrival of an overdue baby. It is a well-known aid to toning the uterus prior to birth, but don't start drinking it until your baby's due date because it may bring on contractions. Consult your health professional if in doubt.

YOU WILL NEED:

Raspberry leaf tea or raspberry leaves

Hot water

A mug decorated with five-point stars (a Goddess symbol) or ripe fruit

The wand from your magical toy box

Brew the tea as directed on the package. If you are making your own, the dosage is one teaspoon of dried leaves or one-and-a-half teaspoons fresh leaves per cup. Pour boiling water on the leaves and brew for three minutes. Hold the tip of your wand in the steam and say,

"Venus plant of raspberry,
Give me smooth delivery."

Sip your tea imagining the joy of your baby. Drink it once or twice a day.

DREAM baby

As your pregnancy advances, you may find it more difficult to rest. Baby may move a lot and your increasing size can be awkward. Many discomforts such as cramp and "restless legs" may be caused by dietary deficiencies as your growing baby depletes your resources. Make sure you are eating the right foods to keep your vitamin and mineral intake at the correct level.

In the same way that you will establish a bedtime routine for your baby that spells "sleep," try to adopt the same habit for yourself. Before going to bed, have a bath to relax, followed by a herbal tea such as chamomile. Practice conscious relaxation of every part of your body, tensing each muscle in turn and then letting it go limp, until your limbs are as floppy as a sleeping kitten's.

Meditation will also help, and if you precede this by your relaxation routine, you will find that you get better results and that it is an excellent preparation for sleep. You need your rest when you are doing the most important job there is—baby-making.

Inward journey for rest and exploration

You can record the following on a tape if you are intending to use this as an exploration rather than for relaxation. Otherwise, memorize the instructions to meander into sleep.

You are standing amid a great field of lavender bushes. Away from you, as far as you can see, there is a lilac haze where the flowers stretch to the horizon. Dappled by the misty sunlight, they climb the gentle slopes of the hills to meet with the hazy blue of the sky. [*Pause to look around*]

Be very careful when using essential oils during pregnancy since many can be dangerous. Always consult a qualified aromatherapist. For massage, dilute two drops of essential oil in one teaspoon of carrier oil, such as grapeseed.

LAVENDER • the best and safest relaxant of all, it can be used to scent bath water, in a burner, or as a massage oil

ORANGE • invigorates and helps digestion

PEPPERMINT • helps with nausea and headaches (safe after 16 weeks)

PATCHOULI • strong and earthy, brings common sense to help anxiety

CLARY SAGE • tones the uterus and stimulates contractions (use this only in the last two weeks of pregnancy and during the birth)

BERGAMOT • energizes and lifts the spirits

NEROLI • relieves depression, treats stretch marks

YLANG-YLANG • good for high blood pressure and stress

TEA TREE • antiseptic

You start walking through the lavender, and as you do so, your clothes brush the spikes, releasing the sublime fragrance. Butterflies flutter over the lavender flowers and there is birdsong from a nearby wood. You find your feet on a narrow track through the field, going toward the wood. Walk slowly toward it. You can hear the lavender stems swishing as your clothes brush them. Walk at a leisurely pace, listening to the rhythmic swish-swish and your footsteps on the springy earth. Take as long over this as you wish. [*Pause*]

Now you are entering the woodland. Lavender bushes still grow thick about you, releasing their scent as you brush past. Follow the tangled path deeper and deeper into the wood. As you advance, the aroma becomes heavier, like incense, and the birds sing sweetly. [*Pause*]

You find that you are approaching an archway formed from tree branches, overhung by many ivy tendrils, so you cannot see beyond. You approach slowly and, stooping, you push aside the curtain of vegetation. You may choose what lies beyond from the following:

　　a) a happy childhood scene—imagine it in as much detail as possible

　　b) a wonderful place, such as a vacation destination

　　c) a pure fantasy

Any of these can be indulged in for as long as you like, to take you into sleep.

A fourth alternative is to meet a being who has a gift for you. You may speak to this being, you may ask about the gift. You may not get all the answers, and you may have to find out later what the gift means. If you are given a gift, it may well be symbolic. It is a good idea to find a replica of it in the real world, if possible, to keep with you.

If you have used the visualization for this exploration, it is best to note down what happens. You can use the visualization as often as you wish, to make you relaxed.

WELCOMING A

NEW ARRIVAL

YOU'VE ARRIVED!

Everything is different now your baby is here. To you it is enormously different, especially if she is your first child. To the world it makes a tiny, but real difference—a new life has come into being, and it is always a miracle.

You may well feel exhausted and not at all like celebrating. If so, you may prefer to do so at a later date or, better still, let someone else do the organizing. When you have been in the hospital, it is really lovely to have a special homecoming.

A house full of flowers is a great way to welcome baby, and lots of candles create a festive ambience, although they need to be placed with extra attention to safety since you won't want to be bothered clearing up wax or shattered glass. Open some champagne and drink it out of your chalice or christening mug. Dab a drop on baby's forehead, too.

Have some time alone with baby, by the light of one white candle, just feeling deeply satisfied that she is here and all is well. You did it!

Baby's rosemary bush

You will be using the rosemary tree on baby's first birthday (see page 125). That may seem eons away, but time will fly! Rosemary protects, purifies, and aids mental powers. It is a hardy perennial that can grow as high as six feet. It has small flowers of white, pink, or blue. Legend says they were originally white, but turned blue when the Virgin Mary placed her mantle over them. If you can, plant a large, healthy specimen in a sunny position, protected from winds. Alternatively, grow one in a pot indoors.

Affirm baby's connection with the tree, and the fact that she is now "rooted," by placing one of her hairs by its roots, or a pebble with her initial scratched on it, or her birthstone (see pages 60–67), or all of these. Hang a star on one of the branches to signify her arrival, and late on you can decorate it with something appropriate for each of the milestones—first smile, first tooth, first step.

The shrub will grow with baby (however, if for some reason it doesn't grow, then don't worry—just buy another and review the situation and care of the plant).

☆ **AFFIRMING THE ARRIVAL** ☆

It may be hard to believe that this little person is now truly here. Try these little rituals to affirm it.

- *Take baby into each room, ring a bell or shake her rattle, and say, "[Name] is here!"*
- *Place baby's tiny feet on the ground for just a moment*
- *Leave a bowl of spring water in moonlight for an hour, then trace droplets over baby, yourself, your partner, and other members of the household. Say, "The tides of life have brought us fortune." Use the water to feed the rosemary bush (see left) and/or flick it around the nursery with a sprig of mint or rosemary, if you prefer*
- *Baby's possessions will soon be everywhere, never fear. For now, to get her feet "under the table," place a bootee that she has worn under the carpet in each room. Alternatively, tie two bootees together by their ribbon and hang them over a picture frame*

"O joy! That in our embers
Is something that doth live,
That nature yet remembers
What was so fugitive"

ODE ON INTIMATIONS OF IMMORTALITY,
WILLIAM WORDSWORTH (1770–1850)

DADDy'S LITTLE darLing

It is easy for a new dad to feel left out of things. What a new mom needs from her partner is more than support—she needs a strong and reliable "connection" with the adult and stable world. A large part of her identifies with baby. For baby, hunger and discomfort are overwhelming and this can make the whole world feel like a scary place for mom, too.

However, the "tower of strength" role isn't always easy for dad. He may be coping with emotions such as jealousy or fear, of which he is ashamed. He is likely to be tired and stressed, too. He may deal with this by closing off just when he needs to be at his most responsive and supportive.

As a new mom, it really is too much to expect that you should handle your partner's emotions, too. Coping with yourself and baby is more than enough. But if you are prepared, there are things you can do to make dad feel good about himself and to bond with the new baby. Once dad's relationship with babe has formed, it has a life of its own and things go more smoothly.

☆ HELPING THE BONDING PROCESS ☆
• Before the birth buy your partner a special gift that has meaning for him
• Hold it between your palms and pour love into it, thinking of all the wonderful experiences you have shared
• Have this ready to give to him just after baby is born
• Have him with you at the birth if it suits you both—show him you need him
• Let him hold baby, bath baby, change baby's diaper, and feed baby as early as possible. If you are breastfeeding, he could give baby a little cooled, boiled water
• Encourage him to play with baby
• Leave him alone with baby

BONDING FATHER AND CHILD

You may like to prepare for this before the birth because afterward, for a while at least, you will have little energy, time, or attention to give to such matters.

YOU WILL NEED:

A pink candle

Sweetpea, jasmine, or rose oil

A piece of rose quartz

A lock of dad's hair

A lock of babe's hair

A small pink bag (this has nothing to do with the sex of your baby). You can make this with pink felt. If you are creative, you may like to make it in a heart shape

Light the candle and heat some of the oil in your burner. Place the rose quartz in front of you. Feel relaxed and harmonious—smile and close your eyes. Think of all the good things about your partner and your child. Let your mind dwell on as many positive images as you can. Take up the two locks of hair and twist them together in a spiral, saying,

"United in love, child and father
Happy together, ever after."

Repeat this if you wish—three times is a good number. Anoint the hair spiral at each end with a little oil—don't worry if it unravels. Place it in the little bag with the rose quartz and put the bag in a location of your choice—possibly under dad's pillow or under the bed.

PART OF the family

A baby—especially a first baby—changes the whole family. A girl becomes a mother, a mother a grandmother, a partner a father. For most people this is a wonderful thing, but not for everyone. Some aren't so keen on their change of status and may find it hard to relate to the new arrival.

Elder siblings may take the coming of a new baby very hard. When my youngest child was born, my third child, just three years old at the time, became fearsome. Although never violent with me or the baby, he terrorized everyone else who as much as looked at his little brother, from doctor to Nana! I was very, very patient with this because I knew inside he was suffering agonies of jealousy. I tried to make him feel as special as I could, but was never sure where it would end. End it did, however, and quite suddenly. As soon as little Ben could lift his head and smile, he adored Adam, and Adam knew it. What he had lost in the attention of everyone else was more than made up for by the delighted gurgles of his younger brother, and he has been his champion and protector ever since.

☆ SIBLING RIVALRY ☆

- *This rivalry is natural—try not to get too tense about it*
- *Plan a special gift for the older child to coincide with babe's birth*
- *Make sure he has something special of his very own, such as a friend or playgroup*
- *Show you respect his toys, his routine, his needs*
- *Try very hard not to be angry with him, however difficult he may be*
- *Arrange times when you can give him all your attention and let someone else handle baby*

☆ FAMILY GATHERINGS ☆

After you have had a baby, you have a right to expect your family to be supportive. However, this doesn't always go as smoothly as it should. Try these magical tips for serene get-togethers.

- *Burn lavender oil in a burner—its fragrance will help everyone to relax*
- *If available, have several bowls of fragrant hyacinths around the room—pink or white are best*
- *Keep the gathering fairly short*
- *Give everyone the baby to hold*
- *Strew dried gardenia around the room before everyone arrives*
- *Put an amethyst geode in the living room*
- *As you prepare food and drink, have an amethyst geode or several unpolished amethyst stones in a purple dish nearby. Pass the refreshments over the amethyst before serving, affirming that the peace of the stone is entering them*

FAMILY BONDING

To make sure your little darling is taken to the bosom of the family, try this spell.

YOU WILL NEED:

Small photos of everyone concerned including baby

A background on which to stick the photos (or use a frame that takes several photos)

Glue or some other form of adhesive

Green or blue thread

Lavender oil

Glue baby's picture in the center of the cardboard and group the other photos around it, sticking on lengths of thread to connect the photos in a network. Anoint the edges of the poster with lavender oil. If there is a particular person who is a problem, move their picture closer to baby (but remember, it is unwise to attempt to manipulate others by magic). You might also glue symbols along the threads, for example, a heart for a more loving relationship. You can experiment with ways of doing this so that it looks attractive.

PROTECTING your Little DARLING

Being a mom brings out every woman's protective side. We all brave things for our children, fight for our children in ways we would probably not consider doing for ourselves. Motherhood awakens the tigress in us.

However, we cannot always be watchful, or even be aware of all the things that might threaten the wellbeing of our child. Sometimes we have to trust in the bounty of the Cosmos to protect our little darling. The right ritual will strengthen your connection with the powers of light and make you feel more secure, so that even if you are parted from your child, when leaving her with a sitter, for example, you are still there in spirit.

☆ **PROTECTIVE STONES** ☆

When you carry out the ritual on the opposite page, you may want to use one of the following protective stones instead of the quartz crystal: agate • amber • apache tear • carnelian • emerald • holey stone • obsidian • ruby • tiger's eye • topaz Other protective symbols could be used instead, for example, a five-point star or an equal-armed cross—or the symbol you discovered in your protective symbol meditation (see page 17).

FINDING EXTRA PROTECTION

To get yourself and your child some extra protection from the subtle realms, it is worth putting some effort into this ritual. This is not a spell to do with baby—get someone else to look after her while you put your energies into it. You may prefer to replace the quartz crystal with another stone (see opposite page) or you may have a stone already that you would like to "charge up" to help protect your little one. Put the stone on a chain and wear it in order to keep both of you safe.

YOU WILL NEED:

A large, flat stone

Your Goddess figure

Two white candles

A feather

Incense/joss stick of frankincense

A red candle

Chalice or christening cup

A piece of clear quartz crystal

Salt

A pitcher of water

A small drawstring bag

Wine or juice

Cinnamon cookies

A wand

Place your stone in the rough direction of north in your working area. Put your Goddess figure behind it with the two white candles on either side of her. (In the Southern Hemisphere, it is best to place this in the direction of south.) Place the feather and the incense in the east and put the red candle in the south (or north, in the Southern Hemisphere). Put your chalice or christening cup in the west. Place your crystal on top of your flat stone. Light the candles.

Form a circle around you as described on page 13. Dissolve some salt in the water and sprinkle the circle with it. Affirm that all negativity is being cleansed from your circle. Imagine it being sucked out, like dust by a vacuum cleaner. Pick up the crystal and rub some salt water over it. Affirm that it, too, is cleansed.

Hold your crystal over the stone and say, "Powers of Earth, give strong and enduring protection." Hold it over the feather and say, "Powers of Air, give versatile protection, from all directions." Hold it over the red candle and say, "Powers of Fire, drive away and consume all harmful influences." Over the chalice say, "Powers of Water, give protection of wisdom and instinct."

Sit in your circle facing your Goddess and hold the crystal on your lap. Imagine there is an egg of light expanding from the crystal until it totally envelopes you and extends beyond you. Hold the image for as long as you can—affirm that this crystal is a generator for a sphere of light, through which nothing harmful can penetrate. Place your stone in the center of your circle and put the crystal on it. Take up one of the white candles and take it all around the circle, starting in the east, and say, "By the powers of sun, moon, land, and sea, this crystal will protect my child ... [*Babe's name*]. So shall it be." Imagine the candle sealing the sphere of light.

Put the crystal in the drawstring bag. Sit facing your Goddess and give thanks. Drink some wine or juice and eat a cinnamon cookie. When you are ready, hold your wand and consciously tell your circle to fade. Extinguish the candles and incense.

Keep the crystal near baby (but well out of her reach) when you feel she needs extra protection. Of course, the crystal will also protect you. You can "charge up" more than one crystal if you like.

BYE BYE, blues

We've all heard about the baby blues. Two or three days or so after the longed-for event, often coinciding with the establishment of the flow of milk, new moms tend to get tearful. This can range from a little sentimental weeping to full-blown depression.

Why should this be? Of course, it's due to the hormones. But more is at work. I well remember the overwhelming nature of several realizations after the birth of my first child, Daniel. I would never again be my own person. There would always be something more precious than myself outside my body. I was connected to the cycles of Life and the process of Time. Nothing would ever be the same again, and nothing I had read or heard in pre-natal classes had given me a hint of this. My tiny, black-haired elf, weighing in at only 4 lb. 6 oz. (little more than 2 kg) was miles away in an incubator, and I was sore all over from a forceps delivery. Being a new mom is cosmic—but it can feel like a black hole.

Your blues will be personal to you. Maybe they focus on your birth experience, circumstances, or the baby himself. Possibly they are nameless angst, misery, or mere anticlimax. If they are severe and enduring, you should not hesitate to get medical help. Otherwise, try this little bathing spell.

☆ BLUES BUSTERS ☆

• *Don't feel you have to struggle alone—talk to someone*
• *Never be ashamed of how you feel*
• *Get some sunshine on your skin*
• *Get out in the fresh air*
• *Ask for help with baby, especially if you have problems*
• *If you aren't breast-feeding, try St. John's Wort tea (check with your practitioner if you are)*
• *The scents of lavender, lily of the valley, and hyacinth promote happiness*
• *Remember you are exhausted and this is bound to make you feel low*
• *Remember you won't always feel like this—things will get better!*

BANISHING THE BLUES

Turn your daily bath into a handy ritual that will help you rid yourself of negative thoughts and feelings and make you smile inside.

YOU WILL NEED:

An oil burner

Orange oil

Several thick orange candles

A large, soft orange towel

An orange, peeled and segmented

As many orange accessories as you like, to reflect in the water

Run your usual salt bath that you will be taking daily after the birth. It is unwise to use any bath oil at this stage, although if you perform this spell at a later date, you may like to use some orange bath oil, to turn your bath water a cheerful color. Orange is a wonderfully invigorating scent, but the essential oil can provoke allergy so avoid touching it. Heat it in your oil burner so the fragrance fills the bathroom, and light the candles so they are reflected in the water. Make sure your fluffy towel is waiting nearby, preferably on a warm radiator, and that someone else is looking after baby so you will not be disturbed. Lower yourself into the warm water. Luxuriate. Say three times,

"Waters of life, wash away my sadness and bring me wisdom and peace."

Feel the water drawing the "blues" from your mind and body. Now, eat the orange and say,

"Brightness, warmth, sunshine, be within me. May I be blessed."

Stay in the bath until you are ready to get out. Wrap yourself in the comfort of your towel and watch your blues spiral down the plughole. Bye, bye.

HELPFUL herbs

Herbs are a distillation of Nature's gifts. There is a special magic to these powerful and useful plants, each with its own personality and essence. When we ingest herbs, we gain more than the chemical components of the plant—we also absorb some of the subtle essence of the plant, its "structural information," and its magical meanings.

Many prescribed and over-the-counter drugs are derived from herbs—for instance, aspirin, or salycilic acid, comes from the willow. It can be argued that drugs are more reliable than the plant source because the components are regulated, whereas plants vary. However, there may be a lot more to it than meets the eye. Plants are living, as we are living, and a certain rapport exists that a pill cannot reproduce.

However, herbs are potent things and their power should never be underestimated. Some medicinal herbs are unsuitable for use during pregnancy; some can even kill if taken unwisely. Always treat these plants with respect and consult an herbalist for specialized advice.

☆ HERBS AND BABE'S AILMENTS ☆

Caution: use a very weak herbal mixture for babies

DIAPER RASH • *rub avocado skin on the rash. Apply powdered goldenseal to a clean diaper. Use marigold ointment. Rub in a few drops of lavender or one drop of rose essential oil in one teaspoon of peach carrier oil (you can use this also as a prophylactic)*

VOMITING • *massage babe's tummy with lavender or chamomile oil diluted in a carrier oil (one drop of essential oil in one teaspoon of carrier oil). Give a little chamomile tea to an older baby, alternatively, let him chew on a piece of apple that has turned brown*

SLEEPING PROBLEMS • *a little lavender oil sprinkled on a clean handkerchief and tied to the leg of the crib will help baby sleep*

CRADLE CAP • *apply mashed avocado to the scalp. Rub in some olive oil, leave all night, and wash off in the morning. Massage with one drop of lavender oil diluted in one teaspoon of light carrier oil. Rinse the scalp with an infusion of meadowsweet*

COLIC • *caraway water can be given to a very young babe if diluted and given in a sterilized bottle. Rub a small amount of diluted fennel oil into babe's tummy before he feeds*

HERBAL HEALING

It is advisable to consult a herbalist for specialist advice before taking any herbs during pregnancy as some are best avoided at this time.

PARSLEY • This well-known herb is ruled by Mercury. Eating it will aid conception. It is also protective—the Romans slipped it beneath their togas to keep them safe. If you are in love, do not cut parsley or it will sever the ties! Parsley essential oil is a little too strong for the nursery and should be avoided in pregnancy, but it may be burned during labour and can be used to treat hemorrhoids and bruising after delivery.

SAGE • Ruled by Jupiter, this herb has—as you'd expect—links with wisdom. If you have a secret desire, write it on a sage leaf and sleep with it under your pillow for three nights. If you dream of your wish it will materialize. If not, bury the leaf in the garden and wish for something else. Cold sage tea, drunk every few hours, usually dries up breast milk. Avoid it during pregnancy.

ROSEMARY • Ruled by the Sun, this herb strengthens the mind, heals, and promotes sleep. To cure "baby blues," wrap powdered rosemary leaves in linen and tie them to your right arm. Rosemary attracts elves. Avoid large quantities of the herb when you are expecting. To boost circulation when pregnant, add 15 drops of the essential oil to your bath water. For backache, use the essential oil in massage.

THYME • This Venus-ruled herb is healing and promotes sleep and love. Wear a sprig of it to see fairies. Large doses should be avoided in pregnancy. A thyme syrup and/or chest rub is great for infants' coughs.

MINT • Ruled by Venus (or some say Mercury), this herb protects, cleanses, and aids travel and healing. As a cleansing spell for the nursery, use a sprig of mint to sprinkle a little salt water around. Leave mint in the nursery for protection. Large doses should be avoided in pregnancy, although a little peppermint can help alleviate the heartburn from which many pregnant women suffer.

a NAMING CEREMONY for your baby

You may be among the growing ranks of people who very much want to make social and spiritual recognition of the birth of their baby without involving any formal religious creed. If so, you can mark the unique gift that is your babe in your own way with a naming ceremony in the presence of selected friends and family.

Performing the ceremony

You can adapt this ceremony to suit your own beliefs and preferences—see opposite for ideas. For the basic ceremony you will need three bowls—one containing water, one containing wine, and one containing lavender oil diluted in water (two drops of oil per teaspoon of water). For an older baby you might use a carrier oil such as grapeseed instead of water. You will also need a large chalice of wine or juice, or individual glasses.

A chosen participant (probably one parent, while the other holds the baby) says, "We celebrate the new life of this precious child. We name her/him ... (*in honor of ...*). May her/his journey upon the Earth be blessed."

The child is then anointed (very sparingly in the case of a tiny baby) on the feet with the water, with the words, "[*Babe's Name*], may you walk in the ways of kindness;" on the chest with the words, "May your heart beat pure and true;" and on the forehead with the words, "May your thoughts flow clearly and peacefully."

Anoint in the same way with the wine saying, "[*Babe's Name*], may you walk the paths of joy;" "May your heart beat warm with love;" and "May your thoughts be positive and inspired."

Do the same with the lavender oil saying, "[*Babe's Name*], may you walk the paths of the blessed"; "May your heart be open to all Creation"; and "May your mind seek the Spirit in all things."

The chalice is now passed around, and each person takes a sip (or they drink from their individual glass). As they do this, they make a wish for the baby in front of the group. Gifts are now given and general celebration follows.

'A good name is rather to be chosen than great riches'

PROVERBS 22:1 KING JAMES BIBLE

Here are some things to consider when planning your baby's naming ceremony.

GIFTS FOR YOUR BABY • You may like to give your baby gifts symbolic of the four elements, Earth, Fire, Air, and Water such as, respectively, a semiprecious stone, a silver candlestick, wind chimes, and a cup. You could plant a sapling, adopt a dolphin, or make a gift to charity. If funds are tight, you may wish to keep your gift very small, but it will feel good to have something to mark your baby's official naming.

MUSIC • Include your choice of music, if you wish. There may be a song that everybody could sing, or simply some recorded music in the background.

LOCATION • Your ceremony can be held in your own living room, a meeting room, hotel, or outside in a garden, woodland, or stone circle. If you are holding it indoors, decorate the room with fragrant flowers and lots of white candles. You may like to strew jasmine or rose petals on the floor. Photographs of ancestors, living or deceased, may be placed in silver frames.

GOD/DESS PARENTS • By all means have several of these if you wish. Make a space in the ceremony for each of them to read out a small poem, pledge an offering for the baby (for example, "I will teach him/her to play the piano if s/he so wishes"), or do something else of their own choice. They may merely state, "I stand as Guardian to [*Babe's Name*]."

GODS AND GODDESSES • If you have a favorite God or Goddess, you may like to have a statue of them close by and ask specifically for the gifts of that deity to be bestowed upon your baby, for instance, Thoth or Athene for wisdom or Kuan Yin for compassion. Light a candle as an offering as you speak.

THANK YOU, WORLD!

Now that you have your babe safe in your arms, you may want to thank the powers of life for their gift by planting a tree or shrub. You may want to involve other people in your thanking ceremony, although you could do this alone if you preferred—if so, wait until you feel reasonably energetic and get someone else to care for baby.

As most births are less than perfect, you may want to go over all this in your head as you come to terms with your fabulous gift and really start to count your blessings. Try to give yourself as much time as possible for this.

Your "thank you" is both a ceremony and a celebration. Make sure it as enjoyable and fulfilling for yourself as possible.

☆ CELEBRATING LIFE ☆

You do not have to "pay" for your babe—the bounty of the universe is infinite, and in any case you have already put in huge effort. Even so, you may feel good saying an extra "thank you."

- *Spread the word about the Goddess, Her value and meanings to those who are interested*
- *Keep an effigy or representation of your Goddess with you, for example, a stone*
- *Plant seeds or a tree (see opposite page)*
- *Give to a children's or environmental charity*
- *Give yourself a treat like a manicure, pedicure, or beauty treatment, as a celebration*
- *Realize what a vibrant part of Creation you are, especially now you have had a baby*
- *Resolve at the end of the day to make a list of all the good things that have happened, however tiny*
- *Buy flowers and light a candle as a small thank you*

Tree-planting ceremony

When you hold your new baby in your arms, it may seem as if your whole soul is saying a big "thank you" to the Universe for this incredible gift. At times like this it often feels good to express emotions in a small ritual and to feel you are giving something back. Why not show your gratitude by planting a shrub or small tree in honor of your babe?

Choose a type of tree that is suitable for the soil and site in which you intend to plant it. Select a hardy specimen and plant it in your own yard, if you can. However, if this isn't possible, it will be just as meaningful if your tree roots in common land.

Involve friends and family in what you are doing. Ask everyone to bring a small amount of soil. Dig the hole and plant the tree according to the instructions. As you place the tree in its hole say, "I plant this tree in honor of ... [*Babe's Name*] and as a thank you to the Great Mother [*or whatever divine being you believe in*] for the great gift we have been given. May we all be blessed."

Babe's parents should place the first handfuls of earth around the roots of the tree, then let the guests add theirs giving a blessing as they do. Bed the tree in, then hold hands around it for a moment. Pass around a big cup of wine or juice and give a drop to the tree, too.

"Her ways are ways of pleasantness, and all her paths are peace."

<small>PROVERBS 3:17
KING JAMES AUTHORISED VERSION, 1611</small>

GETTING TO

KNOw yOu

your TALENTED tiddler

Of course you will do everything you can to make the future as wonderful as possible for your baby. However "magical" you are, there is no substitute for taking practical action, and no doubt you will be on the watch for anything that can help your child to realize his full potential. A little extra is always an asset, and a spell for baby's future will give him that special "something" in life. Use the power of your love to send a message into the ether with these two spells.

Naturally, your baby's future will be up to him. It would not be right to interfere with his own power to choose, so these spells are non-specific. They are simply a way of sending a message to the Universe to say that your babe is special and that you are going to help him as much as you can to realize his dreams. In that way, all your dreams will come true.

You will also be stimulating your babe's awareness for he is bonded with you at a deep level. If you feel excited and hopeful, this is sure to rub off on him. The world is his oyster.

KALEIDOSCOPE OF DREAMS

For this spell you will need a kaleidoscope—it can be as cheap and cheerful as you like. Kaleidoscopes aren't generally suitable for children under three years old because they can easily break into small parts. However, under your supervision you can let baby play with his, so that his personal signature is on it.

YOU WILL NEED:
Jasmine oil
An oil burner
A kaleidoscope

This spell should be performed after baby has gone to sleep. Heat some jasmine oil in your burner and sit beside baby, listening to his even breathing and letting yourself go all dreamy, along with him. Imagine all the wonderful opportunities he will have, all the talents he will develop. Don't concentrate on anything specific—just imagine doors opening for him.

Hold the kaleidoscope up and look within it. Admire all the colors. Turn the funnel and whisper,

"Many colors, yours to shape
Take my love, make your life great."

Say this three times, or more if you wish. Put the kaleidoscope well out of the reach of your little babe and have sweet dreams about the achievements of your little genius.

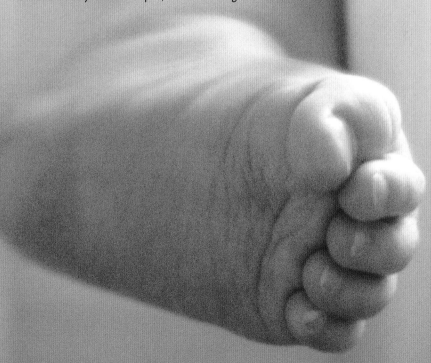

TWINKLETOES

This is an adaptation of an old nursery rhyme that you can repeat at any time as you tweak his toes, one at a time.

YOU WILL NEED:

A white candle

Cinnamon oil

An oil burner

A bell or baby's rattle

When you do this for the first time, make a ceremony of it. Light a white candle and heat some cinnamon oil in a burner. Ring a bell around the room or let your baby shake his rattle hard to clear the air and get things moving.

Let your mind play on all the things your baby could do—don't dwell on any one thing, even if your dearest wish is that he should become a concert pianist or follow in the family business! Just visualize him carrying all before him as he follows his ambitions, and imagine him happy, fulfilled, and successful in his chosen way.

After you have finished visualizing, say the following rhyme—you can both giggle as much as you like.

> "This little piggy went into commerce
> This little piggy stayed home
> This little piggy had a profession
> This little piggy wrote a tome
> And this little piggy said,
> 'Wee, wee, wee—I can be anything I want to be!'"

When you have finished, blow out the candle together and imagine the energy being released into the Cosmos. Repeat the rhyme a couple of times if you like. After this, whenever you say the rhyme, you will recall the more ritualistic times you did the spell, and visualizing will become easier.

> *"A good book is the precious life-blood of a master spirit, embalmed and treasured up on purpose to a life beyond life"*
>
> AEROPAGITICA, JOHN MILTON (1608–1674)

BOOK of DREAMS

Keeping a close record of your baby's first year or two is well worth the trouble. Time passes so fast, things change so rapidly. Those magic moments may be lost to memory unless you have a reminder.

When my children were born, I kept a Baby Book for each of them. It helped me to feel grounded in the reality of this incredible new life and to enjoy all that happened all the more intensely. For this I used one of the specially produced baby books that you can buy in most large bookshops. If you like, you can buy a plain book, leaving yourself scope to enter anything you wish. I did find, however, that having categories, reminders, and spaces for photos helped me to focus.

Be clear what you want to do with your baby book. Is it your own private record? If so, you can feel free to put down all your feelings about motherhood, birth, and so on. Personally I kept these in a separate journal and only put things in the baby book that I was happy to have made public. It's up to you.

☆ WHAT TO PUT IN YOUR
BABY BOOK ☆

- *A lock of baby's hair*
- *Baby's hospital bracelet*
- *Pressed flower from bouquet*
- *Ribbon from her first bootee*
- *A copy of her birth certificate*
- *A photo taken just after birth*
- *A selection of other photos*
- *An account of the naming ceremony*
- *Family customs, traditions, lineage*
- *Inoculations, infant illnesses*
- *List of all presents and cards and who gave them*
- *List of visitors*
- *Details of achievements, for example first smile, with dates*
- *Spells you have done for baby*
- *Baby's tastes, preferences, habits*
- *First Christmas*
- *First birthday*
- *Mom and dad's feelings*
- *Reactions of relatives and siblings*

CONSECRATING YOUR BABY BOOK

Consecration means "making sacred." A ritual to consecrate your baby book is yet another way of thanking the Cosmos for your babe. It will also make your book extra special and draw good happenings to be recorded in its pages.

YOU WILL NEED:

An earthenware bowl filled with dry soil

A lavender-scented joss stick

A white candle

Your chalice or christening mug filled with spring water

A dark blue velvet cloth

Touch the baby book on one corner with a little soil. Say,

"I consecrate this precious book with the power of the rich Earth. May it prove a true and treasured record."

Now, turn the book to the next corner in a clockwise direction and pass this corner through the incense vapor from the joss stick. Say,

"I consecrate this book with the power of the fragrant Air. May it be a clear and entertaining account."

Turn the book again and pass the next corner over the candle flame and say,

"I consecrate this book by the power of the vibrant flame. May it inspire and make happy those who read it."

Once more turn the book and pass it over the chalice or cup saying,

"I consecrate this book by the power of peaceful Water. May it carry the gifts of memory and peace."

Place the four elements in a square formation, with Earth roughly in the north, Air in the east, Fire in the south, and Water in the west (reverse Earth and Fire in the Southern Hemisphere). Place the book in the middle with the appropriate corner toward the element that blessed it. Leave it there for a while as the candle burns down (don't leave the candle unattended). Empty the water on the ground and scatter the soil, then bury the remains of the joss stick and candle. Wrap your book in the cloth and treasure it.

a STAR iS BORN

The art of astrology is as old as civilization. Figures from 17,000 years ago marking the lunar phases have been found by archeologists, and the ancient Greeks had a sophisticated system of reading the stars. True astrology uses a chart of the entire Heavens, drawn up for the time of birth. But luckily all you need is your baby's birth date to know the sign where the Sun was on that important day. The "star sign" is, in fact, the "Sun sign." Astrologers will tell you that the sign containing the Sun is very important for the personality.

The signs come in four groups of three, each of Fire, Earth, Air, and Water. Signs of the same element are similar in character. To help your babe connect especially with his element, or develop an affinity with another element, read about the other elements as well. Baby may well be fascinated by another element—my earthy little Virgo, for instance, adores water. It's all about exploring and finding balance.

BIRTHSTONE SPELL

There are many traditions for birthstones for the Fire signs, but none is definitive—these are suitable suggestions but go with what you feel. For Aries choose ruby or garnet; for Leo, diamond or amber; and for Sagittarius suggestions include amethyst or alexandrite.

YOU WILL NEED:

A gemstone

A cinnamon-scented joss stick

A velvet pouch

Four votive candles

Choose a gemstone that you feel is special and "right." When the Moon is full, burn the cinnamon joss stick. Place your gemstone on top of the velvet pouch and surround it with four lighted votives. Say,

"I bless this stone with the power of Fire. It shall hold luck, love and strength for ... [*Babe's Name*]."

Or use words of your own. Visualize the stone glowing with the fire deep inside. When you are ready, extinguish the candles and put the stone in its pouch as a talisman for your fortunate baby.

Fire signs

Generally, fire signs are impulsive, energetic, intuitive, creative, impatient, and self-important. At their best, great fun, at their worst, a challenge. Although your baby is too young to display this, Fire signs are focused on what is possible rather than actual.

Aries (sign of the ram)—March 21 to April 20

This little one can be a feisty Ram indeed, or more like a lost lamb. But once he's sure what he wants, brace yourself! Make sure little Ram has plenty of baby-sized challenges to use up his energy. Tantrums are a sign of his strength—so just relax. He has a will of iron, but he makes you feel alive.

☆ **FIRE BABY TIPS** ☆

- *Give him plenty of stimulation and as much freedom as you can*
- *Don't try and force him into a mold—especially if you are an Earth sign*
- *He may not notice as much as other babes when he's cold or hungry, so be watchful*
- *Give scope for his imagination and creativity—he may seem chaotic, but you'll see results later in life*

Leo (sign of the lion)—July 24 to August 23

Make way for His Majesty the Baby! He loves to be the center of attention. Don't put him down—encourage his developing skills such as learning how to clap. He's warm, sunny, and affectionate—and bossy from day one. But, oh, how special he'll make you feel!

Sagittarius (sign of the archer)—November 23 to December 22

Life is an adventure, and little Sag will need his own battalion of Guardian Angels as he takes it by storm. Try to restrain him from biting off more than he can chew. Take him out as much as possible, just so he can experience the wonderful world. There will never be a dull moment.

HEAVEN comes to EARTH

If your baby is born with the sun in a different element from yours, you may find her more difficult to understand. If you are familiar with your entire birthchart, you will have even more insight and you may be aware that although your Sun signs are very different, there are other points of similarity.

My fourth child is a Virgo, and I have no Earth at all in my chart. This has meant that some things about him have been a surprise to me. He notices details and is very tactile, needing things that I don't readily provide, such as a defined routine. When he's ill, everyone knows about it, in contrast to my Fire and Air sign children who will ignore any illness as much as they can.

Knowing your babe's star sign is not about putting her in a pigeonhole—it is about looking out for characteristics that you might otherwise have missed or not valued. It is also about encouraging her to explore and develop her full potential.

BIRTHSTONE SPELL

There is no one "right" birthstone—here are some tradition-based suggestions for Earth signs, but always go with what you feel is right: Taurus—emerald or jade; Virgo—agate or aventurine; for Capricorn choose onyx or apache tear.

YOU WILL NEED:

A large, flat stone

A patchouli-scented joss stick

A gemstone

A velvet pouch

Before doing this spell, take a leisurely walk with baby and pick up a large, flat stone that has a pleasant and very solid feel to it. When the moon is full, burn a joss stick of patchouli, put the stone you have collected on the windowsill in the moonlight, and put the birthstone on top of it. Say,

"I bless this stone with the power of Earth. It shall hold serenity, wellbeing and wisdom for ... [Babe's Name]."

Or use your own words. Visualize the power of Mother Earth going into the birthstone, empowering it, making it rich and precious. When you are ready, put the birthstone in a velvet pouch. Return the large stone to the outdoors or put it on your household altar/shrine, if you have one.

Earth signs

Generally, these three signs are identified with their bodies—sensuous, tactile, constructive, and practical. At their best, these individuals are reassuring to have around; at their worst, they may make you impatient. Their minds tend to be anchored in the here-and-now, which can be both inspiring and restricting.

Taurus (sign of the bull)—April 21 to May 21

All babes need security, but with little Bull snuggles are tops! She loves routine and her favorite teddy. She's particularly aware of things that feel or smell nice. You'll think she's an angel—until you try to push her! Stubborn is her middle name, but she may be artistic or musical from an early age.

☆ EARTH BABY TIPS ☆

• *Make sure everything feels especially soft and comfortable—cut off labels, tumble dry towels to fluff them up, choose everything for its "feel" and be aware of subtle scents*
• *Routine is important for all babes, but it is especially so for Earth signs*
• *These babes are very aware of their bodily needs, so respect this—you may not know best!*

Virgo (sign of the virgin)—August 24 to September 23

Here we have a babe who can be hard to please. No scratchy diapers or unfamiliar food—and change that routine if you dare! In infancy she may be delicate, but grows up hale and hearty. She loves to stroke your clothes and hair. She may tidy her toys, and when she's affectionate you know she means it.

Capricorn (sign of the goat)—December 23 to January 20

Cappy has "old soul" written on her baby brow. She may be anxious about life, but she'll still grapple with it. Encourage her to try new things, for she may underestimate herself. She needs predictability and structure. Sometimes she may not be as delighted as you expect, but she's probably placid.

A gift from ON HIGH

Although most people show the traits of their Sun sign, many astrologers believe that the Sun is something we "grow into" rather than instinctively express. So the Sun sign of your baby is likely to become more evident as he gets older.

The age at which the Sun sign characteristics become obvious depends on the individual. My Aries always took life at the double and had far more accidents to the head than the others—and the sign Aries is especially associated with the head. Little Libra could never make up his mind when offered two choices.

Our Sun sign attributes may be what we aim for—young Libra often fears he has not been "fair" or likeable enough, for instance. Your child may need gentle encouragement to value and develop their Sun sign gifts as soon as they begin to move about and talk.

BIRTHSTONE SPELL

There is no one definitive birthstone. Here are some suggestions for Air signs, based on tradition: for Gemini choose agate or aventurine; Libra— lapis lazuli or turquoise; and for Aquarius try aquamarine or jet.

YOU WILL NEED:

A feather or windblown seed

A lavender-scented joss stick

A gemstone

A velvet pouch

Choose a windy day at Full Moon for this spell, if you can. Go for a walk and try to find a feather or windblown seed—or you can collect or buy feathers beforehand, if you prefer.

As the Moon rises, light a lavender joss stick and place the birthstone on or near the feather/s. If possible, open the window to let in the fresh air. Say,

"I bless this stone with the power of air. It shall hold truth, wisdom and beauty for ... [*Babe's Name*]."

Visualize the freshness of the air permeating the stone, making it light and beautiful. When you are ready, place the stone in a velvet pouch along with the feather/s or seeds if you wish.

Air signs

Babe's born under an air sign may be the most communicative, and even if he doesn't talk early, he's especially switched on to what adults around him are saying. He hates fights and tantrums (except his own) and may have an extra need for fresh air in order to feel free.

Aquarius (sign of the water bearer)—January 21 to February 19

Little Aquarius is a law unto himself, and he can't be tied to your routine, only one he decides on. He isn't being awkward on purpose. He loves the open air and meeting people, so take him out and about, but don't expect him always to react in the same way. His quick mind will become more obvious as he grows.

☆ AIR BABY TIPS ☆
- *Include him in adult events as soon as you can*
- *Always behave in a civilized manner when you are in his company*
- *Try intellectual and electronic toys as soon as possible, such as push-button ones that speak the alphabet and mini computers*

Gemini (sign of the twins)—May 22 to June 21

His first word is "Why," so make sure you have an answer ready. He may settle better if he can hear voices. He may prefer a baby sling to a buggy because he can see everything. Keep an eye on the home computer and the phone—he'll be taking them apart. Talk to him as much as possible, he understands more than you think.

Libra (sign of the balance)—September 24 to October 23

All babies are adorable, but Libra is on a mission to charm and make you smile. He loves nice things to look at, so decorate the nursery with special care and find out what music he likes—it'll work wonders. He loves parties—let him hand around the nibbles as soon as he can toddle! Help him to make choices, or you'll be there all day.

wATER baby

The Zodiac is a circle, and like every circle it has 360 degrees. Each of the 12 signs spans 30 degrees, and it takes the Sun about a month to go through each sign and so to move 30 degrees.

As the Sun goes around the Zodiac, it makes angles or "aspects" to the position it was in when your baby was born. The most important angles are the 90-degree angle (square), the 180-degree angle (opposition), and the 120-degree angle (trine).

Squares will happen at three and nine months after birth, trines at four and eight months, and opposition at six months, roughly around the same date as her birth. These may be important times for her. Has she made a leap in understanding? Moved more, started to crawl, been especially restless or happy? Look out for your babe's reaction at these key times and help her if you can.

BIRTHSTONE SPELL

There is no one "right" birthstone. Here are some tradition-based suggestions for Water babies: for Cancer there is moonstone and beryl; Scorpio has bloodstone and tourmalated quartz; for Pisces choose amethyst or labradorite.

YOU WILL NEED:

A jasmine-scented joss stick

Spring water

A chalice, christening mug, or large seashell

A gemstone

A turquoise or purple towel

A velvet pouch

This spell is best performed when the Moon is Full. Light a jasmine-scented joss stick, place your spring water in its chosen vessel (chalice, christening mug, or seashell), and leave it in the moonlight for one hour, if possible. Drop the birthstone in the water and say,

"I bless this stone with the power of Water. It shall give peace, health, and happiness to ... [*Babe's Name*]."

When you are ready, dry the stone on a turquoise or purple towel and store it in a velvet pouch.

Water signs

Water babies are the most emotional and home-loving. They often sense how you feel and may react to your mood even if you are sure you've concealed it. They evaluate life by family bonds and a feeling that everyone cares—not just for baby, but for each other.

Pisces (sign of the fishes)—February 20 to March 20

She's psychic the moment she's born so don't be surprised if everything you think and feel stares right back at you from the cradle. She's probably sensing things that you cannot, so be patient with her tears. Never crush that imagination—she has a touch of Otherworld, which will make her creative later on in life.

☆ **WATER BABY TIPS** ☆
- *Try to keep calm—she'll sense it if you are upset*
- *If she doesn't like a person or place, bear in mind she may know something you don't*
- *If she cries more than others, don't worry about it—it's not your fault. All you need to do is cuddle her*

Cancer (sign of the crab)—June 22 to July 23

Cuddly crab likes to be within her family. Lots of things frighten this little one, but don't underestimate her. She won't give up, and she's determined to explore in her own way. Don't worry if her moods are a mystery because your love is all she really needs. When the chips are down, don't be surprised if she's tougher than you expect.

Scorpio (sign of the scorpion)—October 24 to November 22

What you see isn't what you get with little Scorpio. She may seem to be pushing you away; if so, respect her boundaries, but have a heart full of love waiting, if she opens out. She adores puzzles, and her infant intuition will lead her straight to where you've hidden her presents. Her strong will may be a challenge, but later in life it will be an asset.

FABULOUS fire

The element of Fire always seems magical to our eyes—the bright flames pirouetting with their own life. Fire relates to inspiration, passion, creativity, energy, and imagination. When we make an effort to invoke fire within us, we are stimulating our drive, initiative, power to make changes and have bright ideas. Fire relates to substance in its most volatile state, unpredictable and exciting. As an element it helps us to connect with something beyond and to widen our sense of possibilities.

Fire is sadly missing from our centrally-heated homes, and it is very stimulating to welcome it back in. Babies are fascinated by fire, but obviously this can be very dangerous. If you have a fireplace, cover it with a fine-mesh guard and put babe on a soft hearth-rug. He will then experience the fact that fire is hot. If baby is crawling, he will find it uncomfortable to get too close and with your supervision will begin to respect fire. If you have no fireplace indoors, a chiminea on the patio or veranda is a great substitute.

The spirits of Fire are called Salamanders, and they are believed by occultists to leap and dance within the living heart of the flames, although this is on another level of reality. Quite possibly your baby can see them. Honor the Salamanders by looking for "fire pictures" in the glow—who knows what they will reveal to you?

☆ THINGS TO DO ☆

- *Light candles in colored bowls and glasses*
- *Build a fire in a grate or grill*
- *Set off fireworks*
- *Let baby play with your gold jewelry*
- *Dance in the light of the greatest fire of all—the sun*

☆ PLANTS ASSOCIATED ESPECIALLY WITH THE ELEMENT OF FIRE ☆

Many plants associated with Fire are quite pungent. They include garlic, ginger, clove, cinnamon, orange, rosemary, pepper, basil, bay, and St. John's Wort. Make these into bunches tied with red ribbon and let baby sniff them. They may be too stimulating for prolonged contact, however.

CALLING UPON THE ELEMENT OF FIRE

This is a spell to contact the Fire element and draw on its power, energy, and inspiration.
Why not use this whenever you and babe need zest for life and new ideas for playtime?

YOU WILL NEED:

Several red candles

Cinnamon oil

An oil burner

Lively music

A packet of sparklers—preferably of different colors

Red wine or juice

Light the candles, heat the oil, and play the music as loud as your baby finds comfortable. Dance if you like. Let baby watch the flickering flames.

Light a red sparkler and write "energy," "drive," or "inspiration," or a similar word in the air three times. Finish off with "Blessed be." Do the same with a yellow sparkler writing, "swift thought," "communication," or "bright ideas." With a blue one write, "harmony in the home," "peace," or "kindness." With an orange one write, "happiness," "laughter," or "celebration;" with green write, "health" or "luck;" and with white write, "purity" or "fresh starts." If there are only white sparklers, use them for all of the above.

Finish each set of wishes with, "Blessed be." Let baby hold the sparkler with your hand over his if you feel you can do this safely—naturally you will be very careful. Sip some wine or juice—you have spelled it out for the Salamanders.

celebrating the ELEMENT OF EARTH

In magical terms the element of Earth equates with protection, feeling grounded, physical sustenance, fertility, and all things practical. When we make an effort to connect with Earth, in a subtle fashion we are stimulating our ability to be in harmony with the material world, to enjoy its gifts, and to use our common sense. "Earth" relates to substance in its solid state, enduring and preserving. It helps us to identify with our five senses and to enjoy the gifts of our bodies.

Your baby is only beginning to discover what her body can do and feel. She will love to experience this tactile element and through it her own power to make and do. Please don't worry about your baby getting dirty—as long as you are reasonably careful, especially in regard to animals (cat and dog feces are obviously dangerous), all will be fine. There is a school of thought that says young children actually benefit from exposure to some bacteria. Certainly all my children managed to eat earth at some point and did not appear to be harmed!

Getting the gnomes on side

The spirits of Earth are called Gnomes, and occultists believe that they exist on another plane of reality, tending all the things that grow from and within the earth—from flowers to crystals. Maybe your babe can see them among the green stems. Bring your baby with you when you water your plants, sow seeds, or plant cuttings. If you have no garden, tending house plants and windowboxes will suffice. The Gnomes will realize that the Earth has another friend and give her their protection.

☆ **PLANTS ASSOCIATED ESPECIALLY WITH THE ELEMENT OF EARTH** ☆

All plants are sustained by Earth, but some carry its essence more strongly. These include wheat, barley, rye, potato, rhubarb, and the flowers tulip and primrose. Tie bunches of these with green ribbon and place them near baby's cradle to conjure the presence of Earth.

☆ **THINGS TO DO** ☆

- *Let your baby walk barefoot or crawl on soft grass*
- *Supervise your baby playing with sand or clean soil*
- *Encourage baby to touch tree bark, stones, leaves, and flowers*
- *Clothe your babe in natural fabrics such as cotton and choose wooden furniture*

EARTH TALISMAN

This spell will help you connect with the Earth element and benefit from its protection.

YOU WILL NEED:

A small piece of coal

A sturdy green or brown plant pot

Potting medium

A hyacinth bulb

A piece of malachite (a lovely green stone associated with the Earth element)

Place your piece of coal at the bottom of the pot and cover it with fresh medium. Let your baby touch some of the soil, running it over her fingers. Plant the hyacinth bulb, again involving baby as much as you can. This could get messy so put down some newspaper, or better still do it outside. Press down the soil using baby's little hands. Now press the malachite into the soil. Say,

"I plant this flower in honor of Life. Earth, always protect my child."

Look after the bulb as it grows and flowers. Hyacinths are said to prevent nightmares, so if you have a large, airy nursery, you might choose to have it on baby's windowsill. When the flower has passed its best, take out the malachite and treasure it—it is a protective talisman of Earth for your child.

LIGHT AS AIR

The element of Air relates to communication, thought, movement, and all that is light and free. It is connected to reason, theories, and everything hatched in the mind. When we lift ourselves up into the airy realms, we are liberated from our feelings and able to let our thoughts take flight. Air relates to substances in their gaseous state, impossible to hold or confine. It can help us expand our minds, to be detached, impartial, inspired, and liberated. It can also give us words, ideas, new perspectives, and freedom.

We cannot see this subtle element, only its effects. Your baby may be fascinated by leaves blowing in the wind and strong gusts that take his breath away. What he will certainly be aware of are scents. Through the medium of scent, Air brings us a whole spectrum of information about our surroundings that affect our brains. When baby catches your familiar scent, it has an immediate effect on his mind, worth a thousand words.

The spirits of the Air are the Sylphs. They ride upon the breeze and keep the atmosphere mobile and clean. Could baby be aware of them? His thoughts are free and his eyes undimmed by any preconception—the Sylphs love that.

☆ THINGS TO DO ☆
• *Take a walk up a breezy hillside with baby in a sling*
• *Look for cloud pictures*
• *Watch birds—leave out scraps to tempt them into your garden*
• *Fly a kite*
• *Play with balloons*

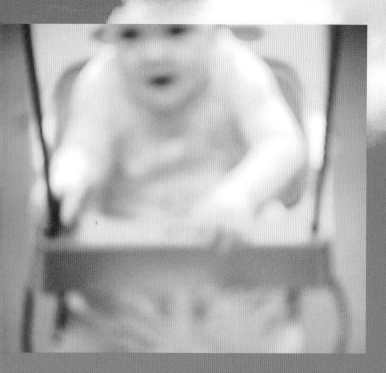

☆ PLANTS ASSOCIATED ESPECIALLY WITH THE ELEMENT OF AIR ☆
Plants need oxygen to grow, reaching blindly up into the fresh air, offering their leaves to the birds and the breezes. Some have a particular affinity with Air. These include lavender, mint, parsley, lily of the valley, hazel, broom, and orange bergamot. Lavender can be placed among baby's clothes to keep them sweet.

BRINGING AIR TO LIFE

This spell will help to keep your mind clear and your thoughts inspired. It will also help to pep up your social life.

YOU WILL NEED:

Wind chimes (choose some that you especially like the sound of, some can sound tinny)

Salt

Lavender oil

Cleanse the wind chimes with salt water. If you are worried that they will rust, just rub a little salt over them—this is intended to be a symbolic and subtle cleansing of any influences carried over from the shop where they were bought. Imagine all impurities being washed away.

Think about all the communications you would like to come for you and your baby, through the post, by email, or by telephone. Think about visitors, friends, contacts, people to chat to. Think about baby's growing recognition of speech and about his first words, soon to be uttered, about his developing brain, his ability to move, crawl, walk, and the purity and clarity of his outlook. Ask that this be preserved and ask that the communication, people, and baby's progress be drawn to you as you anoint the wind chimes with a little lavender oil on each funnel.

Hang the wind chimes in the east of your home if you can. If the air is quite still, let baby play with the chimes, so the air comes alive with the sound, singing out a welcome to the Sylphs with their gifts. Do this whenever you feel you and baby are stagnating—you'll soon be ringing change!

bewitching wATER

It is well known that the sea, when it appears in dreams, tends to signify overwhelming emotion. Water is the element of feeling. It relates to tribal bonds, empathy, sympathy, healing, and generally feeling connected to the people—and possibly things—about us through the way we feel. Water also cleanses and transforms. Although gentle, it has an inexorable quality, as when the ocean erodes granite. Water relates to substances in their liquid state, taking on the shape of a container, but easily slipping through our fingers. Water can help us make emotional bonds, understand our heritage, and tune into the needs and feelings of others.

Your baby started life in the waters of the womb. This was her universe, here she developed, suspended and nourished, with the incessant beating of your heart her call to consciousness. Most tiny babies really love water and can readily be taught to swim. They know no fear of this familiar medium. Bath time, too, is a source of joy and mirth. The feeling and behavior of water is often a source of endless fascination to tots and older children, too.

The spirits of Water are called the Undines. They play and ride upon the waves or linger by the shores of lakes or oceans, singing strange and beautiful melodies that sometimes you may just catch as a far-off echo. Your baby will hear this song and will be aware that the water is alive and filled with magic.

☆ **THINGS TO DO** ☆

- *Swim with baby*
- *Take baths with baby*
- *Catch raindrops*
- *Wade*
- *Play in a wading pool in the yard*
- *Take baby in the shower with you*
- *Let baby play with spring water, where it comes out of the ground, to have contact with the element at its purest*

☆ PLANTS ASSOCIATED ESPECIALLY WITH THE ELEMENT OF WATER ☆

All plants need Water to survive, but some are more potently connected with its essence. Willow, apple, lemon balm, columbine, cowslip, eucalyptus, gardenia, jasmine, pansy, sweet pea, violet, yew. A bunch of some of these may be placed in the nursery, tied with a blue, purple, or turquoise ribbon, to invite the fresh yet mysterious element of Water to be present.

SPELL FOR THE ELEMENT OF WATER

Water has some amazing properties, and there are New Age theories and "fringe" science that state that water can be altered by our thoughts. Some writers, for example, the dowser T. C. Lethbridge, said that psychic phenomena usually cluster around places where there is a significant water content below the soil, or where there are streams and lakes. This is because water holds psychic impressions, like a film.

YOU WILL NEED:

A purple candle

Pure spring water (please note, the spring water should be from a reliable source that you know and trust and should be used as soon as the bottle is opened because spring water can cause food poisoning)

A chalice or christening cup

A cheesecloth cover

Full Moon may be best for this spell, which should be carried out shortly before you go to bed. Light the candle and sit looking at it for a while, sorting out in your mind the special wishes you intend to manifest for your baby. Keep this fairly simple—after all, you can do this spell as often as you like. Pour the spring water into the chalice and sit with it on your knee, holding it gently between your palms. Visualize what you want for your baby very clearly as you hold the chalice. Imagine the power of your visualizing going into the water, so that it appears in the water, like a film. Do this for as long as you feel comfortable.

Cover the chalice with the cheesecloth and leave it by your bed overnight. In the morning, give a little to baby on a spoon. Let her be nourished by your dreams and watch them come true.

folk MAGIC

Not so very long ago, life was harder than we can imagine. There was little help for the infertile, apart from magic, and many babies were born dead or died in infancy from infectious diseases. In medieval times the life expectancy of a woman did not extend beyond her early twenties. This was in great part due to the dangers of childbirth, which ended the lives of many women. Small wonder that endless charms and customs arose in an attempt to give at least the illusion of control of the forces over life and death. However, a spell is more than just a superstition—it is a way of focusing the unconscious mind. Who knows how many folk customs worked because people believed they would?

There are customs linked to trees and standing stones. For instance, not far from where I live in Somerset, England, stands Minchinhampton Holey Stone. In days of yore, children who had measles were reputedly passed through the hole in the stone to heal them (although it looks too small to me). Men-an-tol in Cornwall, southwestern England, served the same function. In respect of trees, the ash was believed to cure rupture or rickets. The tree was split, and the child passed through it nine times. After this the life of the child depended on the continuing life of the tree.

You may like to research old customs in your neighborhood. If you find anything that appeals, why not try it for the wellbeing of your babe? We now have more reliable ways of healing, but observing local customs may help your child connect with the subtle energies of the land on which you live.

"...Custom calls me to't
What custom wills, in all things should we do't,
The dust on antique time would lie unswept,
And mountainous error be too highly heaped
For truth to o'erpeer"
CORIOLANUS, WILLIAM SHAKESPEARE (1564–1616)

☆ EASING CHILDBIRTH ☆

- In mountain areas of the U.S., red corn cobs were burned near a woman in labor to ease travail
- In Iran, pregnant women wore saffron under their swollen bellies to bring speedy delivery
- Hyacinths were believed to ease childbirth and could be dried and kept in a cheesecloth bag for the purpose
- Powdered amber was burned to ease childbirth

☆ MAGIC FOR BABIES ☆

- Pregnant women would eat quince to guarantee the baby would be very clever
- Birch was considered a fertile and cleansing tree and was used to make cradles to confer magical safety
- In Aargau in Switzerland, when a boy was born an apple tree was planted and when a girl was born a pear tree was planted. The child was then believed to thrive or not, in unison with the tree
- Coral, given as a gift to a child, will ensure his future health, and coral beads are said to ease the pain of teething
- A holey stone (a naturally occurring stone with a hole) may be hung over the babe's crib with a red ribbon, for protection
- In North Africa, alum is placed in the headdress of children as protection
- In India, lapis lazuli is strung on gold and hung around infants' necks to protect them
- Garlic placed beneath a child's pillow will protect him
- A sachet of caraway seeds placed in babe's bed protects him from illness

☆ FERTILITY SPELLS ☆

- A piece of rowan was tied together with birch twigs and placed over doors to attract fertility
- In Northern India, the coconut is sacred to the Goddess Lakshmi and is given to would-be mothers by the priests
- The women of the Kara-Kirghiz would roll on the ground beneath an apple tree to become pregnant
- Bringing home the may was a fertility rite performed at the start of the month of May in England. This resulted in babies being conceived then and there in the Greenwood. Dancing around the maypole was also a rite for fertility
- In India, women wear a perfect white diamond with a slightly black background for a male child

EVERyDAy

mAGIC

morning MAGIC

Thank the Goddess for the morning. Somehow
everything is more manageable when that promising
light comes creeping in. When my children were tiny
babies, I half-dreaded nighttime, when I knew I would
be exhausted, yet unable to sleep properly because
of baby's demands. Often we both slept best at the
approach of dawn for a few blissful hours.

When morning comes, you may want to let it right
inside you, so you can also be renewed. Take baby around the house with you and open
all the windows to let the fresh air in, just for a moment if it is cold, and take a deep breath.

Celebrate the morning by slipping on a bright yellow housecoat, sipping tea from a
mug with a sunflower on it, playing with baby with a big yellow ball, and talking to her
about what you're both going to do that day. And if you feel like it, sing. She will love to
hear the sound of your voice.

Ask yourself what is the most important, or most irksome thing on your agenda today.
Get it over with first thing, so you can enjoy the rest of the day with your baby.

☆ MORNING TIPS ☆

*If you have a bad night with baby, you might find it difficult
to get going in the morning. These suggestions might help.*

*TEA • the tea plant is ruled by
the Sun and brings strength
and courage. Your morning cup
of tea contains antioxidants
and folic acid. Green tea, made
from the shoots of the tea plant,
is less stimulating but more
beneficial. Place cold, used tea
bags on your eyes and rest for a
few minutes to ease tiredness
SHOWER • this is more
invigorating than a bath. Use
a non-slip mat and have towels
ready, then you can take baby
in with you—she'll love the
tingling drops*

*HAIR AND MAKEUP • set
aside five minutes in the
morning to do your hair and
makeup—you deserve it
and you'll feel better for it
HOT LEMON • squeeze some
lemon juice into a cup of hot
water to drink first thing in the
morning as a liver tonic and
wake-me-up
BERGAMOT • soap and body
lotion containing oil of
bergamot will make you feel
energized for the day ahead.
Heat some bergamot oil to fill
the room with vitality*

DRESSING BABY

Like so many everyday activities, dressing baby can be turned into a spell if you are switched on to symbolic meanings and use them. Choose the colors of baby's clothes according to how you would like her to be, or what you think she needs and, as you dress her, state the purpose (see below). Why don't you dress to match baby? Together you'll be unbeatable.

WHITE • today you will feel so peaceful and serene/protected from harm/lovely and fresh and clean

BLUE • today you're going to be really peaceful/sleep well/feel better

RED • today you're going to be a bundle of energy (use red with care)

YELLOW • today you're going to be really alert and interested in new things/love traveling

ORANGE • today you are going to be really happy

GREEN • today you will feel soothed and healed/you'll be my little good luck charm/you and I are going to get some money

BROWN • today we're going to feel all homey and cozy/you're going to enjoy meeting some animals

PINK • today you're going to be warm and affectionate, meet friends, and get lots of cuddles (little boys aren't traditionally clothed in pink, but maybe you don't care—anyway, you can get away with a bit of pink in his socks, for example)

baby ON THE MOVE

The open air is very good for your baby. It stimulates his mind and makes him more alert and responsive. He will experience this most happily if he is held in a baby sling where he has the comfort of the closeness with your body to give him confidence. Wind, snow, rain, and sunshine all have their part to play.

In centuries gone by, life was very demanding, and people did not have the option of staying in the warm, hopping from car to front door, never meeting the challenge of the elements. In many ways this was not good, for some babies did not survive such rigors. However, today we go to the other extreme, shielding babies from their birthright—contact with all the moods of Nature.

If you would like your baby to grow up aware of his roots and in touch with his instincts, let him experience the great outdoors.

☆ GOING OUT CHECKLIST ☆

Every new mom knows that taking baby out is like moving house. Streamline it by having an easy-to-carry bag ready packed by the door. Include the following:

- *diapers*
- *baby wipes*
- *soft towel*

(unless your bag has an upholstered section for baby changing)

- *plastic bag for dirty diapers*
- *spare coat*
- *change of clothes*
- *feeding bottle (if you aren't breastfeeding)*

If there are other items you feel you may need but could forget in the confusion of getting ready, keep a note pinned to the refrigerator as a reminder.
Finally, for a little magical protection while you travel, pop a comfrey leaf or some Irish moss into baby's bag.

STROLLER CHARM

A baby sling is ideal if you have concerns for baby's welfare in certain weathers, but obviously you will need a stroller for shopping and ordinary out-and-abouting. Choose your stroller with care, remembering considerations like weight, ease of folding, and interchangeability with car seat. Then give it that extra something with this traveling charm.

YOU WILL NEED:

An indelible felt-tip pen
A yellow drawstring bag
A yellow candle
A pebble
A small feather
Powdered ginger
A small shell
A lavender-scented joss sick

Use the indelible felt-tip pen to draw the symbol of Mercury on the yellow drawstring bag. Mercury is the God of travel and commerce, and his symbol is a circle with a cross beneath (like the "female" symbol), but with an inverted semicircle lying on the top of the circle.

Light the candle. Place the pebble in the bag saying, "Earth, keep my journeys safe." Then put in the feather saying, "Air, speed my journeys." Then put in the ginger saying, "Fire, empower my journeys;" and finally, add the shell saying, "Water, make my journeys peaceful."

Tighten the drawstring, hold the bag, and look at the candle saying, "Mercury, bless all my journeys with my child." Hang the bag from the buggy. Put out the candle—you can keep it to burn again before long journeys, if you wish. Light the joss stick as an offering to Mercury (but do this away from baby as the smoke could be harmful).

friends with the FAIR FOLK

All over the world there are traditions relating to the people of Faerie—beings from another dimension who are sometimes helpful, sometimes tricky, and definitely to be respected. These feature frequently in children's stories. The well-known tale of Rip Van Winkle returning after a short space of time in Faerieland to find a hundred years had passed clearly shows that time runs differently in the land of the faeries.

The Irish call them the People of the Sidhe—the old gods who now dwell within the hollow hills. In Scotland a minister named Robert Kirk (1644–1692) wrote *The Secret Commonwealth of Elves, Fauns and Fairies*— and was subsequently believed to have been abducted by them. The Welsh body of legend, the Mabinogion, is full of faerie lore while other faerie accounts come from around the globe, from Bengal to Peru. One thing most faeries have in common is their fascination with children.

The Fair Folk love the wise, the beautiful, and the young. There exists an old belief in faerie thefts of babies, leaving in their place a changeling. Whether there is any literal truth in these stories or not, there is certainly symbolic meaning. Babies and children still have one foot in Otherworld, and our task is to make sure they keep some of that faerie enchantment by introducing them to magical tales and ideas, but we also need to prevent this from going too far. All that we do in connection with faeries helps to create an atmosphere of magic for baby.

"Up the airy mountain
Down the rushy glen,
We daren't go a-hunting,
For fear of little men"
THE FAIRIES, WILLIAM ALLINGHAM (1824–1889)

☆ TRADITIONAL FAERIE SPELLS ☆

• To see faeries, wear a sprig of thyme
• Blue and red primroses growing in the garden will protect your home and little one from anything evil and attract good faeries
• Roses also attract faeries
• Faeries love to have offerings of milk or food. Leave it outside—especially at Halloween. The faeries will take the essence, not the substance
• Garlic, placed beneath a child's pillow, will keep away all evil
• Peony roots also protect little ones from mischievous sprites
• Faeries hate iron and wearing it will keep them away. Open scissors, hung like a metal cross on baby's crib, will protect her from their attentions
• A daisy chain around your babe's neck will protect her from faeries
• A four-leafed clover is especially lucky and will protect baby from bad faeries while enabling you to see them

MAKING FRIENDS WITH NATURE SPIRITS

A more modern idea is that faeries are nature spirits—beings who empower the land and tend plants and trees. These beings are benevolent, but obviously saddened by the damage we are doing to the environment. This spell will help your babe make friends with a nature spirit.

YOU WILL NEED:

A red or blue primrose in a pot
A green candle

Buy a red or blue primrose in a pot, light a green candle beside it, hold baby on your lap, and talk to the spirit of the plant. You may feel silly while you are doing it, but the great thing is that you have baby with you and so you can pass it off as a game you're playing with her. Involve baby in tending for the plant by watering it (don't overwater) or moving it to a better position, all with baby in tow. Tell the plant spirit that you are bringing up your child to have true respect for all of life. Ask that the spirit of the plant remembers the special bond that you are forging between your babe and the world of Nature.

When you feel the time is right, plant the primrose outside (in your garden, if you can) with a lock of baby's hair under the roots. Ask the plant's spirit to let the message of love between Nature and your babe be spread as far as possible. Be careful not to kill the plant with kindness. However, if it fails to thrive, don't worry. You have still sent out a message of warmth to the plant kingdom. Now you can try again.

hEALING baby

When your baby is ill, it can be one of the worst times in your life. He can't talk to tell you what's the matter and his distress is unbearable. Add to this the fact that you are tired and stressed, and things can very quickly get totally out of proportion.

Obviously you will need professional care if there is something seriously wrong. Trust your intuition and don't be fobbed off for fear of looking foolish if you are anxious. Insist on immediate medical attention or take babe to the ER, if necessary.

Most illnesses, however, are not serious, and the majority of babies have lots of minor ones. If you feel overwhelmed, your partner, mother, or close friend may be able to take over with baby to give you a break. Their more detached and objective perspective will be a great comfort and help.

If you can be relaxed and serene, there is no one better able to heal baby than you, his mother. You are in tune with him, your life force can heal him and ease his discomfort. Trust your instincts as a mom.

"Humpty Dumpty sat on a wall
Humpty Dumpty had a great fall
All the king's horses
And all the king's men
Couldn't put Humpty together again"
TRADITIONAL NURSERY RHYME

HEALING HELP

This is an all-purpose spell that you can do outside the room while someone else is looking after your snuffly, unsettled little darling.

YOU WILL NEED:
Lavender oil
Eucalyptus oil
A green candle

Have a relaxing bath yourself and add some lavender oil to the water. Rub the eucalyptus oil into the candle and light it. Now sit quietly, watching the flame. As you do so, imagine baby all relaxed, happy, totally well, and peaceful. Hold this image for as long as you can—really believe it. Imagine the green color of the candle enveloping baby in a soothing aura. Say the following lines three times,

"Thriving, smiling—by my spell
Babe of mine, you're happy and well."

When you are ready, blow out the candle and release the spell. Repeat this as often as you like until babe is better.

HANDS-ON HEALING

If you are calm and "tuned in," you will be able to sense how baby is feeling. With three of my children I found I could always tell, if I managed to still the clamor of my own brain, just how serious the problem was. With my eldest, who was premature and seriously ill, I could never trust my instinct—the early rupture in our relationship had made me unsure of myself. A mother's intuition, when it is intact, is the strongest there is.

Visualize a white-gold halo over your head, feel very calm, and lay your hands on baby's tummy. Probably you will feel in your own body what he is feeling. You will get a sense of how strong or weak he is, how hot he is, and whether he is in pain.

Visualize the halo over your head becoming more brilliant and this light going into you, empowering you. Feel this power gathering behind your navel and traveling down your arms. Let your hands be guided to the place on baby's body that needs soothing. Feel your palms tingling as the power travels down into them and transfers itself to baby. Visualize the light converting to whatever color you feel is needed to heal baby—green and blue are both very soothing colors and help to ease pain. You can imagine the pain being wrapped up by them and neutralized. Sometimes, however, you may feel a vibrant color like gold or orange is what baby needs, to soothe colic for instance. Go with what you feel is best. Soon babe and you will be getting some much-needed rest.

mAGiCAL moveMeNt

Dancing with baby is a very special experience. It gives your babe a chance to relive some of the time spent in the womb when she moved with you, within the amniotic paradise. Babies will often respond especially well to music they heard *in utero*. Besides, dancing with baby gives you a wonderful opportunity to listen to music in peace, knowing baby is with you and you are catering to her needs, while enjoying yourself. It is also a great way to get fit after the birth.

With my third child, Adam, I adopted many of the practices of the Continuum Concept. Anthropologist Jean Liedloff wrote a book by this name that is based on the lifestyle of the Yequana Indians. It involves holding baby for a lot of the time. As my first two children were considerably older at the time, I had the opportunity to do this with Adam, walking, dancing, and even propping him next to me in the kitchen while I worked. He is now a particularly poised and coordinated nine year old, possibly because he learned from my movement how to be in tune with his own body.

As you hold baby, you will become very aware of her responses. Maybe you could let this lead you on to experiencing new types of music that baby might like. Dancing with baby won't necessarily make her develop into Margot Fonteyn, but it will certainly help her enjoy life and find her own creative response. Music has been said by some to be the most spiritual of the arts because it is pure vibration, of which the Universe is composed. Experiencing music with your babe can unite you on many levels.

"Energy is Eternal Delight"

The Marriage of Heaven and Hell,
William Blake (1757–1827)

DANCING FOR BABY'S FORTUNE

With this spell you seal the love between you and the bonds that will always be there, even when baby grows up. The music symbolizes the ether, through which loving hearts are always in close contact.

YOU WILL NEED:

An instrumental music CD or cassette with soft, rhythmic music

Hold baby and start to sway. Say,

"You and I step together
Tied in love forever and ever
Music swing and music flow
Round and round and round we go."

Hold baby away from you and say,

"You and I step apart
You are always in my heart
In this dance I give you joy and health
Love and mirth, wisdom and wealth."

Repeat the last two lines as many times as you wish.

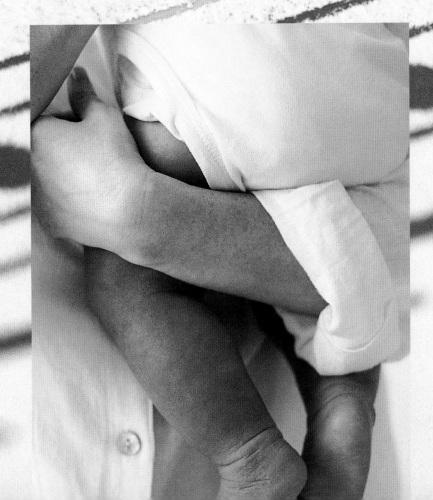

PLAY, LAUGH, and LEARN

Babies and children learn through play. In their playing they test out the world, their own talents and abilities, and learn to stretch their understanding and potential. Indeed, play is a very serious business. People who were encouraged to play when young grow into the most creative and imaginative people who really make things happen.

Peekaboo is one of the first games your babe will play. He has come to know and love the contours of your face. By appearing and disappearing you are, in fact, teaching him a very important lesson—that things that go also come back. The reason for all that giggling and excitement is that tiny grain of fear that you *won't* reappear. In testing out what this might be like, babe is taking the very first step toward processing separations as an adult.

The more varied and funny you can make this game, the more you will both enjoy it. If baby gets upset, you have found the limit of his ability to process, for the moment. The same applies if he gets bored. Give him a cuddle and try again some days later, taking it slowly. Peekaboo should make you both laugh and laugh—a great way to unwind if you've been stressed all day.

☆ **VARYING PLAYTIME FUN** ☆

Remember that play is a serious business that helps your babe progress. Here are one or two ideas for playtime.

- *Play peekaboo with teddy and other favorite toys*
- *Try popping back wearing different hats or a scarf or a towel over your head*
- *Try covering baby's face with his sheet—he will soon get used to pulling it down to surprise you!*
- *Throwing a ball backward and forward will help hand–eye coordination, even if babe drops it*
- *Anything you do that makes eye contact with baby helps his development*
- *Sing to baby. Anything that has sudden, funny sounds like "Pop Goes the Weasel" should make him giggle*
- *Wear tough, clean jewelry—baby loves to grab anything shiny, and it helps his concentration*

PEEKABOO SPELL

*All that laughter that you and baby are enjoying is actually a kind of power—
and this power can be used in magic. Choose a time of day to do the spell when
you know you have time to yourselves and always follow it by something
relaxing like a bath or feed and then a nap.*

YOU WILL NEED:
A white candle

You can light a white candle before you do this spell if you like, just to set the scene. Make sure baby is comfortable and in the mood. Start to play, repeating the following rhyme,

"Peekaboo, peekaboo, I love you
Peekaboo, peekaboo, just we two
When you are grown
And away have flown
You'll always remember peekaboo—boo!"

You can make funny noises along with the verse if you like. Keep playing and upping the excitement, just to the right pitch. Imagine the giggles rising like bubbles and gathering above baby. When you are ready, stop playing. Imagine the "bubbles" contain all your dreams of a confident and talented future for him. Hold him and blow out the candle—as you do so, imagine the "bubbles" being blown into the ether and popping their power to make your wish come true. Enjoy a relaxing, cuddlesome time together.

troublesome TEETHING

There is something very special about that first, pearly tooth. Usually it appears around six months. It shows your baby is developing and that Nature, despite any worries you may have, is working her usual magic.

However, teething can be very unpleasant for some babies, making them tearful, restless, and generally tetchy, and even gives some runny stools. A classic sign is a red patch on one cheek.

There are over-the-counter applications that you can buy, but you may be wary of these. Folk remedies usually come from pure sources, more in keeping with the purity of your babe's own body. Being unadulterated, they lend themselves more readily to a little magic.

To empower your healing remedies, consult Hands-on Healing (see page 87), where you will have read about building up a glow behind your navel and sending this down your arms to heal baby. Place the remedy (see list opposite) in front of you, close your eyes, and imagine the glow going down your arms making your palms warm. Hold your hands over the remedy, palms downward, and imagine the power of the life-force flowing into the remedy. Imagine baby feeling better. Do this for as long as is comfortable and then apply the remedy.

"For there was never yet philosopher
That could endure the toothache patiently"
MUCH ADO ABOUT NOTHING, WILLIAM SHAKESPEARE (1564–1616)

☆ TRADITIONAL REMEDIES ☆

• *Massage the affected cheek with oil of chamomile—dilute two drops of the essential oil in one teaspoon of carrier oil, such as grapeseed or sweet almond. (Be very careful to avoid baby's eyes and test first for allergy)*

• *Make a chamomile compress. Fill a bowl with warm water, add six drops of chamomile oil, and soak a clean cloth in this solution. Then apply to babe's cheek*

• *Let baby chew on a stick of carrot. However, do not leave her alone for fear of choking. Carrot is ruled by Mars and may pep up a listless babe*

• *The homeopathic remedies belladonna, calcium carbonate, and calcium phosphate are recommended for teething. Homeopathy works on a different principle from herbalism, using minute amounts of a substance that might cause the problem to "inoculate" against it. Homeopathic remedies are available now in many pharmacies and health-food stores. For more information, consult a homeopath*

• *Coral beads worn around the neck were said to help teething. However, such as necklace could be very dangerous, so try some magically charged coral beneath baby's crib instead. To charge it, see page 45*

LICORICE RELIEF

Chewing licorice root is said to be a cure for teething. Licorice is ruled by Venus and is a lovely way to impart soothing and love to your baby. You should be able to buy licorice sticks at your local health-food store.

YOU WILL NEED:
Licorice sticks

Empower the licorice stick in the same way described for the other remedies (see opposite page). Now, holding the stick, make circles counterclockwise around your baby's head—probably she will be very interested in this and try to grab the stick. As you circle, imagine that you are gathering up the pain and inflammation, rather like cotton candy clings to a stick, and then flick it away with a movement of your wrist, over the top of baby's head. Do this for as long as feels right. Don't give this stick to babe to chew, however—give her a fresh one that you have also filled with your love.

a place for pApA

As your baby grows, there will be more and more ways for daddy to play his part. He may feel that he can more readily relate to a little one that smiles and grabs his finger. As playmate and protector he has a special function. He is not as close to the emotional realm as mom, so he can more readily inject fun and humor.

Try to make sure your partner does as much baby-care as is fair, depending on how you have apportioned the bread-winning and household tasks. As baby grows up, dad will get an unforgettable buzz from helping that very first crawling attempt, the first step, first word, and so on. These are all moments to treasure, and dad will only have those memories if he is taking part.

☆ HELP NEEDED ☆

Once baby starts moving, he'll be quicker than you can imagine, and you will never know when he will suddenly develop a new skill. There are so many things that will need to be done around the house, and your partner will feel needed if you let him know how much you value his attention to them. If he's no handyman, maybe he can organize someone else to step in to do these tasks.

- *Put child locks on kitchen cupboards, the fridge, and toilet seat*
- *Install a stairgate*
- *Cover stove burners*
- *Make sure all unused electrical sockets are covered*
- *Put corner protectors on all sharp edges*

- *Tuck away trailing electric cords and/or clip them to the wall*
- *Reorganize breakables so they are out of reach*
- *Keep the floor free of all small objects*
- *Empty trash*
- *Keep all sharp objects safely put away in drawers*

BOOST THE BONDING

Dad may need reminding that he has his own special bond with baby, one which has nothing to do with anyone else.

YOU WILL NEED:

A deep pink candle

A photograph of just your partner and child

A deep pink photograph frame

A small sprig of fresh rosemary or a pinch of dried rosemary

Light the candle and sit quietly for a while, imagining a strong and loving bond between your two special people. Remember all the happy moments you have seen them share.

Place the photograph in the frame with the rosemary behind it and close it up. Place the frame by the candle and say,

"Laughter and closeness these two, whatever,
Knowing joy in life together."

Let the candle burn for a while. Leave the photo where your partner can see it regularly (a small photograph in a cloth frame could be stuck to the car dashboard, for example). If you wish, you could repeat this spell for more than one photograph.

FEEDING fortunes

Feeding baby should be a joy for both of you, but for some reason this is very often not the case. There can be problems with mom's supply of milk, or baby can be uncooperative and unable to suck. Sometimes all seems okay, but baby doesn't thrive as she should and the bottle seems the only alternative. In old times there would have been a wet nurse to step in. Modern moms may well feel that formula is a better option than to witness another woman suckling their baby.

Despite trying my hardest, breastfeeding did not work for me. It was very upsetting, because I am committed to things being as natural as possible. I went through so much that my midwife almost begged me to stop. I began to see that getting upset was not good for my baby and settled for a peaceful, comfortable bottle and feeds I could look forward to instead of dreading.

If you are one of those lucky people for whom all goes smoothly, you may find breastfeeding "cosmic" and one of the most magical things your body can do. If you have problems, rest assured you are certainly not alone. There are several things you can do to make feeding more special for you and baby.

☆ GETTING CLOSE
WITH BOTTLE FEEDING ☆

• Loosen your clothing and hold baby skin-to-skin while giving her her bottle
• Warm the milk to body heat by placing the bottle between your breasts half an hour before babe feeds
• Hold the bottle, close your eyes, and pour your love and strength into it—do this by visualizing a glow behind your navel (see Hands-on Healing page 87)

☆ TRADITIONAL AIDS
FOR BREASTFEEDING ☆

• Infusions of caraway, dill, fennel, and aniseed promote the flow of milk. Use one teaspoon dried herb or one-and-a-half teaspoons fresh herb per cup. Brew for three minutes and take three times a day
• Echinacea will help any infection
• Lavender oil in a bath can reduce the let-down effect
• Chamomile and calendula essential oils will ease painful breasts. Wipe off remnants before feeding
• Calendula cream is effective, too, and safe for baby to swallow
• Engorgement can be helped by applying a paste made from powdered marshmallow root and cold water. Let dry, wash off, and repeat every 2–3 hours

EASY LACTATION

All around the world the clear quartz crystal was considered a "milk stone." Isis would be a good choice of Goddess for this spell because of her motherly dedication to the infant Horus.

YOU WILL NEED:

As large a quartz crystal as you can comfortably wear, cut in a smooth oval or lozenge shape, and hung on a silver chain

A white candle

Gardenia or jasmine oil

An oil burner

Your favorite Goddess figure

A velvet cloth

Perform this spell before the birth so you can time it with Full Moon. Go to your nearest freshwater spring and hold the crystal in the flowing water. Say,

"May this crystal be cleansed by Mother Earth and may my milk flow as freely as her springs."

When the Moon is Full, light your candle and heat your oil with your Goddess figure in front of you. Hold the crystal in your open hands, towards the Moon. Think of the power the Moon has to swell the tides, her whiteness, roundness, and the light that spills from her. Say,

"Lady Moon, give me your blessing. May my breasts grow full with milk, may it flow pure as your light, abundant as the tides which obey your command."

Feel the light of the Moon pouring into your crystal, filling it with power. Leave the crystal by your Goddess figure in the moonlight for several hours. Before dawn, wrap it in a velvet cloth and pledge an offering to your Goddess, such as a gift to a children's charity. Wear your crystal as the birth approaches and afterward to make your milk flow abundantly and easily.

BATHTIME bliss

Bathing baby is a special time for you both. Most babies love the water, and it is a chance for you enjoy each other's company and to play. When baby is very tiny, you will be concentrating on supporting his head and being very gentle. But he will soon grow and start to respond and splash.

The practicalities of bathing are very important. Make sure you assemble everything you need first, as you won't be able to leave baby once he's immersed. If your bathroom is large enough, it is best to have a semi-permanent baby bath on a stand that you can fill from a shower nozzle to make it much easier on your back.

Best of all, get in the bath with baby. I found this great fun when mine were little. Install a nonslip bath mat for safety, and make sure you have a big, soft terrycloth robe ready to slip over you as soon as you get out because you'll have to attend to babe immediately.

"Bobby Shafto's gone to sea
Silver buckles at his knee;
He'll come back and marry me,
Bonny Bobby Shafto!"

Songs for the Nursery, 1805

☆ TIPS FOR A MAGICAL BATH ☆

• A little lavender essence helps "psychic" cleansing and sleep. Because it is so gentle, a few drops in the water should be fine for all but the tiniest babies.

• As you wash, imagine anything negative being washed away, too. For instance, if baby has been grouchy or not well, imagine this being washed off as gray gunge and sucked down the plug-hole.

• It is possible to buy special body paints for use in the bath. You and baby can have great fun painting on and washing off. Try a tiger's face or clown's red nose.

• Invest in some really luxurious towels to finish off. Choose the color of the towels for their symbolic associations—what do you want to be wrapped in? Red for courage and energy, blue for peace, purple for spirituality, yellow for creativity, orange or gold for cheerfulness, green for healing and prosperity, pink for affection, white for purity and happiness, or brown for a homey feel.

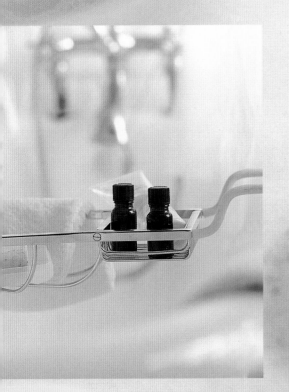

BLOWING BUBBLES

You can do this spell at any time, but it is good to do it in the bath where there is plenty of water and you can enjoy a special time all to yourselves. Baby really needs to be able to sit to get the most from this and give you free hands. Light as many candles as you can in the bathroom so that the light is reflected in each bubble, or let in the sun if it is daytime.

YOU WILL NEED:

One of the small pots with its special wand for bubbles that you can buy in any toy shop

Several candles if it's dark, or let in the sun during the day

Blow cascades of bright bubbles, topping up the water with babe's own bath water. Say,

"Bubbles, bubbles, floating free
Take all cares from babe and me
Airy, faerie, light as can be
See how they pop, one two three!"

Visualize everything as light and carefree, that your heart is as light as the bubbles. Baby will try and catch the bubbles—have fun!

magical MOBILE

A mobile can be a powerful charm. On it you can weave your hopes and wishes for baby's future, hanging it over her bed to be there at that most vulnerable time—when she is sleeping. While you sleep, too, your love and care are still with her in the mobile you have made.

The Chinese art of Feng Shui teaches that the life-force or "chi" needs to be able to move freely around a room. If you look at the nursery, you may be able to visualize the movement of chi. Where might it go stagnant or stale (page 22)? This could be a good place for your mobile, as it will enliven the air with its motion.

Making your mobile

To make the basis of the mobile, you will need a strand of wire that is as firm as possible, but you will need to be able to form it into a circle, about 10 inches (25 cm) in diameter. Find a dinner plate, circular cake pan, or a similar item to act as a template. You will need ribbon or cloth to bind around the wire, which you can secure with glue or stitching, and four lengths of ribbon or cord to fasten at equidistant points around the circumference of the circle, so you can suspend the mobile from the ceiling. The length of the ribbons will depend on how low you want the mobile to hang. Needless to say, everything you use needs to be as safe as possible, or carefully secured so there is no possibility of it falling into baby's bed.

Once the basics are complete, it's down to you. Think carefully about all the things you wish for your infant. Try not to be too specific because, after all, you can't know what may be right for your baby in detail. But general blessings such as health, wealth, intelligence, security, love, luck—these are all to be recommended. For each of your "gifts" you will need an emblem, and these can be cut from cardboard, thick felt, molded from self-hardening clay, or anything else you can think of. Love, for example, could be symbolized by a red heart; intelligence by a small scroll; money by plastic toy money; happiness a smiley face; luck a star; health a rosy apple; peace a lunar crescent, and so on. Take your time, allow yourself to dream and add to your mobile, if you wish, as the days go by. Think about the quality you are invoking as you shape or draw the symbol. If you are creative or artistic, you may want to keep to a theme; for example, make all shapes symmetrical, use silver cloth, or make sure all the colors of the rainbow are represented.

DEDICATE YOUR MOBILE

When your mobile is complete, hold a small ceremony to dedicate it. Choose a waxing moon for this spell if possible.

YOU WILL NEED:

White candles

Jasmine or lavender oil

An oil burner

Soft music

Your favorite Goddess effigy

A chalice or christening mug

Wine or juice

Light the candles and heat the oil. Play soft music and touch each emblem on the mobile in turn, visualizing the particular gift it carries and saying, for instance,

"Great Isis [*or Goddess of your choice*], Goddess, mother, wise woman, grant the gift of love [*for example*]."

Repeat this as often as necessary. Hang the mobile, give thanks, and raise a toast to the Goddess.

Your child has a charmed future. Blessed be.

and so to bed

A sleeping baby is one of the most beautiful sights Nature has to offer. Bedtime is a snuggly time, with lots of special contact with your baby. Sometimes, however, it may not go quite as smoothly as you would like. When you are tired, this can be very trying, but do your best to keep calm because your mood will obviously affect baby.

Bedtime ritual

Ritual is a wonderful tool for conditioning the subconscious. Making sure you have a regular, soothing routine is a kind of magic. Get into sleep sequence.

Bath is a lovely precursor to sleep, so bathe babe before bedtime as often as possible. Burn some lavender oil in the nursery prior to bedtime as this will help to soothe and relax. Get in the habit of reading a bedtime story long before your baby can talk, the sound of your voice will be reassuring to him. However, for a tiny baby a bedtime lullaby or rhyme may be better than a story having the effect of a magical chant (see below). Make sure baby has his familiar toys with him in his crib, and try to have bedtime at roughly the same time every evening so baby can get into a routine.

Finally, don't feel bad if it doesn't work. Baby came to earth with a unique personality—keep trying to find something that suits you both.

☆ MAGICAL CHANT ☆

Memorize this repetitive chant to repeat to baby at bedtime. Fit it to a gentle familiar tune if you wish, such as the Christmas carol "Away in a Manger."

"Sleep baby sleep, the sun has gone away
Sleep baby sleep, the stars come out to play
Dream baby dream, your future shines so bright
Dream baby dream, sweet dreams the peaceful night.

Sleep baby sleep, the moon is rising high
Sleep baby sleep, snug in your cot you lie
Dream baby dream, tomorrow bright and new
Dream baby dream, will come with gifts for you."

BABY DREAMCATCHER

Native American traditions tell us that a properly made dreamcatcher can trap nightmares and make sure only sweet dreams get through. Make one for your babe, to guarantee the most peaceful sleep. New Age shops sell them, but for an extra-magical one just for your baby, there is no substitute for your own handiwork.

YOU WILL NEED:

A wooden hoop (available from needlecraft counters), no more than 4¾ inches (12 cm) diameter

Lilac ribbon or seam binding

Glue

Thick lilac thread

A large-eyed needle

Two soft feathers

Silver symbols such as you would hang on a charm bracelet or use to decorate a cake, for example a teddy bear

Play soft music and think of your baby sleeping peacefully with a smile on his face. Wind the lilac ribbon or binding tightly around the hoop and secure with glue or by sewing. Weave a web with the thread from one side of the hoop to the other, making the pattern as complex as you like—it doesn't have to be neat. You can do this by sewing the thread to the binding, or, if the thread is too thick to thread into the needle, tie it securely at the edges. Tie the feathers to two lengths of ribbon and dangle them from one side of the hoop. At the opposite point, tie a ribbon to hang the hoop from the ceiling. Now thread or glue your symbols to the lilac web and your dreamcatcher is ready for action.

Hang the dreamcatcher by the window, well away from your baby's crib. Make very sure that it cannot fall or be blown onto him when the window is open, or, worse still, grabbed by him when he is lying in his cot, because the small parts will be very dangerous.

BABy THROUGH

THE yeAR

LUNAR Little ONES

The Moon is very important to life on earth. Lunar phases have been found marked on artefacts from as far back as 35,000 BC, showing ancient people were aware of her influence. Menstruation has a lunar rhythm, plant metabolism varies with the phases, and the fertility of many animals is connected to the Moon—salmon and horses to name but two. Oysters brought inland on Long Island were found to alter their opening/closing sequence in direct response to the Moon overhead. Pregnancy, which is described as lasting 40 weeks, is actually nine Moons from conception to birth, and according to my midwife, more births tend to occur around Full Moon.

The Moon, of course, moves the tides. Seventy percent of the earth's surface is water, and the same percentage of our bodies is also water. Your baby's sensitive and pure body is likely to be especially responsive to the Moon. The Moon in the birth chart is held by astrologers to be very important in describing our responses, emotions, habits, and instinctive reactions, and many believe that we identify most with our lunar characteristics as babies.

So it is very worthwhile to observe how your babe reacts to the Moon, in order to gain a better understanding of him and of heavenly cycles.

☆ OBSERVING THE EFFECT OF THE MOON ☆

Once you have an idea how the Moon affects your baby, you have your own secret supply of magical information. First, you will need a lunar calendar to tell you the current phase of the moon. You should have one in your magical toy box, but any newspaper will give you this information. You will also need a moon baby diary, which you will need to keep for a couple of months at least before you can be sure whether baby is reacting to the Moon. Make a note the following:

SLEEPING • *does Full Moon keep him awake or Dark Moon make him drowsy all day?*
FEEDING • *is his appetite affected by the Moon?*
WEIGHT • *does he put on weight more easily when the Moon is waxing?*
ENERGY • *when is he on the go, settled, fidgety, or alert?*

MOOD • *does he gurgle and giggle more at certain times of the month or seem especially touchy at others?*
HEALTH • *are there certain times when he seems more likely to be unwell?*
CUDDLES • *does he want to be held more at certain times than at others?*

☆ TRIBAL MOONS ☆

Indigenous peoples have great respect for the Moon. It is vital in the Chinese, Islamic, Hebrew, and Mayan calendars. Certain African tribes look on the Moon as mother, and women celebrate a special rite for fertility and the souls of the dead at the New Moon at the start of the rainy season. Many Native American tribes have a calendar that involves the Moon, with special names for each Full Moon (see below). Why not cut out pictures or press flowers for your Baby Book on these themes? Sing your baby songs, show him pictures, and—above all—let him see the lovely shining Moon.

JANUARY • *Wolf Moon, Play Moon*
FEBRUARY • *Snow Moon, Black Bear Moon*
MARCH • *Crow Moon, Big Clouds Moon*
APRIL • *Seed Moon, Pink Moon*
MAY • *Milk Moon, Flower Moon*
JUNE • *Honey Moon, Rose Moon*

JULY • *Thunder Moon, Mead Moon*
AUGUST • *Corn Moon, Woodcutter's Moon*
SEPTEMBER • *Harvest Moon, Fruit Moon*
OCTOBER • *Hunter's Moon, Basket Moon*
NOVEMBER • *Beaver Moon, Initiate Moon*
DECEMBER • *Long Night Moon, Oak Moon*

MOON baby

It takes the Moon 29½ days to go from Full to dark and back to Full again. Dark Moon is the time when the Moon cannot be seen, about two weeks after Full Moon. Waxing Moon refers to the two weeks when the Moon is growing. She rises later and later in the night until Full Moon, when she is overhead at midnight. Her light coming through the nursery curtains may be enough to waken baby. As the Moon wanes, she is up later and later, until she can be seen, all pale and wan, in the morning, as Dark Moon approaches. Each of these cycles will see considerable changes in your babe.

Not only do the lunar phases affect life on earth, they are also linked to magic. This is understandable for several reasons. Moonlight affects the way we think and perceive—certain chemicals in the brain are more active at nighttime, and we are more receptive to the subtle realms. By moonlight we are more ready to believe in ghosts. Also, some things can be seen better by moonlight. For instance, a candle flame disappears in sunlight, but for the Moon it dances with delight.

The time when the Moon is waxing is, not surprisingly, the time for most magic, especially connected with increase. Full Moon is very magical, while the waning Moon is a time for banishing. Spells to get pregnant belong with waxing and Full Moon, spells to banish anger or similar to waning Moon, while Dark Moon is great for meditating. Ordinary life, too, is regulated by the Moon with substances being more easily absorbed while the Moon is waxing and activity greatest at Full Moon. Of course, the response of your babe is personal to her, so you can adjust accordingly.

☆ **MOON ANGEL** ☆

We all have Guardian Spirits that watch over us and your baby will have her own Guardian Angel. One angel is especially linked to the Moon. His name is Gabriel, which means "Strength of God." In the Bible he appears as a messenger, telling Mary she will bear Jesus. To Mohammed he revealed the Koran. If you need a special message to help you understand your babe, burn some jasmine oil in the nursery or have some fragrant lilies close by. Hold baby and stand together in the light of the Full Moon and listen for Gabriel's message whispered in your ear. Ask Gabriel to strengthen your own babe's Guardian Angel. Close the curtains tightly and sleep peacefully.

☆ ATTUNING BABY TO THE MOON ☆

*• The best time to give older babies a tonic is with a waxing Moon—
her body will absorb it better at that time*

• Baby will probably put on weight better while the Moon waxes

*• Use the high-energy time of waxing and Full Moon to stimulate
your baby with new experiences, new toys, and new activities*

*• If you are weaning and unsure whether a new food will agree with
her, try her with it when the Moon is waning, when her body will
less readily absorb it*

*• Some substances are "ruled" by the Moon—these include silver,
moonstone, crystal, beryl, aquamarine, sapphire, selenite, and pearl.
Let your baby touch them, to get that "lunar vibe"*

*• Take baby out in the moonlight and watch how she reacts. Can
she see things that are invisible to you?*

baby at FULL and DARK MOON

The Full Moon is a wonderful time for so many of the spells in this book. Both you and baby will feel inspired. Baby is not as used to moonlight as you are, and to him it will seem truly magical. Why not celebrate Full Moon by wearing lots of silver jewelry or even a silver coronet? An older baby will love to take his turn at being Moon King, but be careful you don't scare a small babe with strange lunar headgear.

The Moon is especially associated with certain animals, including dog, bear, dolphin, wolf, and snake. Baby may have cuddly versions of several of these. Play with them, making all the appropriate noises, for some Full Moon fun.

Dark Moon is the time for meditation and looking inward. You and baby might not feel as much like going out at this time. Stay quietly at home if you like and have a nap with baby cuddled up close. These are moments to treasure—in years to come he will not so readily settle with you for snuggles.

DARK MOON DREAMING
Do this spell when you and baby are both relaxed and dreamy.

YOU WILL NEED:

A purple candle

A black or dark stone that you have picked up locally

An amethyst

Light the candle and sit comfortably, holding the dark stone. Think about the past month. Are there things you wish you had done differently, especially in regard to baby care? Or do you feel okay? Whatever the case, pour your memories into the stone—feel it grow warm with the energy. That month is gone, and you can build on the good or change the not so good.

Now take up your amethyst and begin imagining how things will be in the coming month. Dream about this in detail—how you will behave, what you will do, the changes and improvements you will make. Daydream as long as you like, until you doze, if you wish. As you dream—so shall it be. Later on, bury the dark stone well away from the house or throw it into a stream.

CATCH A MOONBEAM

*This spell will help with the bonding and gentleness between
parent and child. You will need the light of the Full Moon to do
this spell, but if you are determined to do it in cloudy weather,
a large white or silver candle may be used as a substitute.*

YOU WILL NEED:

Jasmine oil

An oil burner

*A large white or
silver candle
(optional)*

*A large silver or
white bowl filled
with spring water*

Burn the jasmine oil and let the moonlight
(or candlelight) fall upon the surface of the
water. Let baby play with it as you hold him.
Put your own hands in the water so it seems
as if you are cupping the moonbeam. Now
stroke some water on baby's face saying,

"By the light of the Moon above
You and I are joined in love."

An older baby may imitate what you have
done. Have fun! Use the water for your
garden or house plants.

baby with wAXING aNd wANING MOON

As the Moon waxes, it is likely that baby will be more open to new experiences. She may have lots of energy and be especially into everything. This is a great time to go out and about with her, seeing how she reacts to different places and people. If you feel that you have both slid into bad habits, now is the time to change them. If you feel like making creative changes to the nursery, a waxing moon is a great encouragement, so why not put up a new frieze, introduce a soft sheepskin rug, or get a smart new toy box.

Waning moon is a great time for a clear out. Do you have drawers full of baby clothes that no longer fit? Time for them to go to charity, or be stashed in the attic. The closer you get to Dark Moon, the more the two of you are likely to feel like slowing down. Of course, it is possible that you do not follow the pattern and that one or both of you actually feels increasing energy with a waning Moon. If so, go with what you feel.

What if babe has a different response from your own? Well, at least you know. While you are full of beans, it's not a problem. You can sort things out while baby sleeps. However, if it's the other way around, then try to make sure that major jobs are out of the way by the lunar phase when you are at your least energetic, so you can devote what energy you have to baby.

Observing the Moon is really about becoming aware of your, and your baby's, internal rhythms. At this time in your child's life, you are hopefully a little detached from the rat race, so take this opportunity to discover the true benefits of attuning to your instincts.

"Hey, diddle diddle,
The cat and the fiddle
The cow jumped over the moon;
The little dog laughed
To see such sport,
And the dish ran away with the spoon."
FROM *MOTHER GOOSE'S MELODY*, C.1765

*Try this if you have the Baby Blues. Choose the first Saturday
of the waning Moon. Light a black candle and say,
"Old Moon, old Moon, take from me all my cares. Blessed Be."
Relight the candle each evening of the waning Moon until
Dark Moon. Bury any leftover wax in the garden.*

☆ MOON GODDESSES ☆

*To many peoples, such as the Celts, Inuit, Aborigines, and
Japanese, the Moon was masculine and the Sun feminine.
Certain tribes saw the Moon as the "other husband" of women,
responsible for pregnancy. However, Moon is a feminine noun in
French, Spanish, Latin, and Russian. The gentle, cyclical Moon
seems feminine to us.*

*The three aspects of womanhood are Maiden, Mother, and
Crone—the Maiden corresponds to the waxing Moon, the
Mother to Full Moon, and the Crone to Dark Moon.*

*If you have a Goddess altar, you may like to honor these
different Goddess aspects at the phases by placing an effigy there
and lighting a candle. Maiden Goddesses include Persephone
and Artemis; Mother Goddesses are Demeter, Isis, Gaia; and
Crone Goddesses include Hecate, Spider Woman, Kali.
Goddesses such as Kali and Hecate are not truly scary. Many
Goddesses incorporate all three, such as Celtic Bride, Greek Hera,
and Babylonian Ishtar. You may like to research the meanings
of these Goddesses and ask for their blessing for your child.*

☆ WAXING MOON TIPS ☆

*Do the following spells while you are holding baby to bring her
special luck and blessing.*

- *Kiss your hand to the New Moon and make a wish for baby*
- *Make sure you are standing on soft earth or grass, take a good
look at the New Moon in the sky, turn around three times, and
make a wish for baby*
- *When you first see the New Moon in the sky, make sure your
partner is the first person of the opposite sex you see, then kiss
him before you say a word. This will bring you a gift*
- *When you see the New Moon (not through glass), turn over
the change in your purse or pocket to bring you more money
to spend on baby things*

*"In Spring, when woods are getting green
I'll try and tell you what I mean"*

Alice Through the Looking Glass, Lewis Carroll (1832–1898)

Spring Spellwork

In Spring, every day brings something different. The emerald-green shoots, the brilliant flowers, and the ever-lengthening days bring a sense of excitement and optimism. Everywhere the miraculous growth of your baby is reflected in Nature.

At the Spring Equinox, on or around March 21 (September 22 in the Southern Hemisphere), day and night are equal all over the earth, but light is gaining. Welcome this by filling the house with daffodils and primroses, letting baby touch the bright petals. If the sun is shining, stand or sit him on the windowsill to experience the growing warmth.

Easter is named for the Teutonic maid Goddess, Eostre, in whose honor eggs were hidden and found. Easter, which always falls on the Sunday after the first Full Moon after the Spring Equinox, is tied to Nature's cycle. Why not take baby on his first egg hunt? He will pick up on the excitement and shiny wrappers, even if he can't eat the eggs.

MAGICAL EGGS

An egg means new life—your baby came from one!

YOU WILL NEED:

A green candle

A small gift for baby such as a teething ring, rattle, or chick-shaped toy

An egg-shaped box such as you would use to present an Easter gift

A soft green ribbon

Light your candle and think what you would most like to "grow" in baby's life. What does he need? This does not have to be infant-specific—it could be something like a new home or better job for mom or dad. Hold the gift and think about this. Then place it in the "egg" and tie it up with the green ribbon. Leave it on the nursery windowsill overnight, so that the dawn rays can fall upon it. Open it with baby the following morning and say, "Ah, look, here is our charm for [*whatever you chose*]. Aren't we lucky!" Every time baby plays with the toy, the magic will grow.

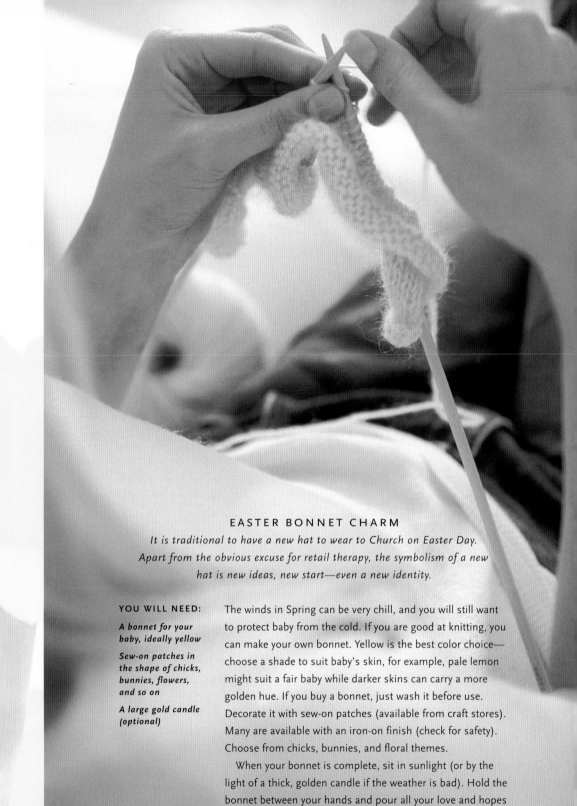

EASTER BONNET CHARM

*It is traditional to have a new hat to wear to Church on Easter Day.
Apart from the obvious excuse for retail therapy, the symbolism of a new
hat is new ideas, new start—even a new identity.*

YOU WILL NEED:

*A bonnet for your
baby, ideally yellow*

*Sew-on patches in
the shape of chicks,
bunnies, flowers,
and so on*

*A large gold candle
(optional)*

The winds in Spring can be very chill, and you will still want
to protect baby from the cold. If you are good at knitting, you
can make your own bonnet. Yellow is the best color choice—
choose a shade to suit baby's skin, for example, pale lemon
might suit a fair baby while darker skins can carry a more
golden hue. If you buy a bonnet, just wash it before use.
Decorate it with sew-on patches (available from craft stores).
Many are available with an iron-on finish (check for safety).
Choose from chicks, bunnies, and floral themes.

When your bonnet is complete, sit in sunlight (or by the
light of a thick, golden candle if the weather is bad). Hold the
bonnet between your hands and pour all your love and hopes
for your babe into it. Feel your hands growing warm with the
power of your thoughts. Wrap babe's head in the bonnet—all
ready for Spring and crowned with love.

here comes SUMMER

The delightful thing about summer is that feeling of freedom that comes from not having to wrap baby up against the cold. When the weather is really warm, she can lie outside in the shade to play with water and watch the butterflies. Burn a natural aromatherapy incense cone close by, but out of her reach, to deter harmful insects.

Folk festivals and fairs are often based on older themes, celebrating light and warmth. All these events may seem more colorful and meaningful now you have your own baby connecting you to the web of life. Take baby out to as many events as you can. Older babies may like to watch clowns or go on a merry-go-round with mom or dad.

Coaxed by the sun, you may feel inspired to go on longer walks. See how baby reacts to strolls under a canopy of green leaves, as the shadows dapple her face, or to the more bracing air of a hilltop. As in Spring, let her smell and touch the luxuriant flowers. Why not add some fresh rose petals to her bathwater, for a summer blessing from Aphrodite, Goddess of beauty?

☆ BABY SUMMER THEMES ☆

- *Bees were believed by the Goddess-worshipping Cretans to be the voice of the Goddess. Baby will love to watch them at work in the flowers. Bumblebees will sting only if cornered, so just make sure she doesn't grab!*
- *Visit fountains and streams*
- *Play with balloons and kites*
- *Discover seashells and pebbles*
- *Independence Day is July 4—celebrate freedom at this time*
- *Set off fireworks in the dusk and let baby sleep under the stars while you have a barbecue*

Beauty baby massage

The Celtic summer began at Beltane, on Mayday, and this festival honored all the sensual gifts of the Goddess. In our culture we are apt to be critical of our bodies—not so your baby! She identifies with her body and all its experiences. Massaging your baby may make her giggle and will stimulate her awareness of the gifts of her body. Later on, as she grows, unconsciously she will carry the memory of being pampered and special.

Essential oils are unsuitable for small babies, so just use a small amount of sweet almond or grapeseed oil. Don't massage her after a feed. Make sure the room is warm, and place babe on a soft towel. Remove any jewelry from your fingers and wrists, and wash your hands.

Massage her all over using the minimum of oil and maintaining eye contact to see what she enjoys most. As you massage, say special words, such as, "I bless your beautiful head, may you carry all before you in life. I bless your perfect hands, may they touch all that is wonderful," and so on. Major on what is pleasurable and beautiful—it is summer, after all. Don't forget baby's feet. Turn her over to do her back and roll her up in the towel afterward, to drowse.

DAISY CHAIN

The daisy is ruled by the planet Venus, and when it is worn, it attracts love. Naturally your baby will already have all the love in your heart, but this spell will help make the whole world adore your little darling.

YOU WILL NEED:
A blanket
Daisies

Spread a blanket on the grass for baby to lie on while you pick some daisies. When you feel you have enough daisies collected, make a tiny slit in each of the stems with your nail. Now thread each daisy through the stem of another until you have a chain long enough to make a necklace. As you do this, feel relaxed and loving—let your thoughts wander over pleasant experiences of love, warmth, and play. When the chain is complete, put it around baby's neck saying, "I garland you with love and beauty." This is fine for boy babies, too, for it's great to be handsome. Cuddle your baby and say a big thank you to the Great Mother.

"Season of mists and mellow fruitfulness
Close bosom friend of the maturing sun;
Conspiring with him how to load and bless
With fruit the vines that round the thatch-eaves run"

ODE TO AUTUMN, JOHN KEATS (1795–1821)

FALL fun

Fall is rich and gentle. Days are misty, soft dusk creeps in earlier and earlier, fruit hangs plump and heavy. The leaves show the first tinges of orange, red, yellow, and gold. At this time you will treasure even more the closeness with your baby. How good it is to hold your own new life, as the trees and hedges are heavy with theirs. And how comforting it is to have your living proof of the future, while outside, everything begins to withdraw below the earth in preparation for winter.

Traditionally, at Fall Equinox, the veil between this world and the world of Spirit is said to be thin and ghosts walk. Do not be afraid, for your baby is not. He may spot them in the lengthening shadows and understand that they are simply disembodied souls that may one day incarnate again upon the earth.

In Celtic tradition, late Fall was the start of the storytelling season. Your babe is too young to understand a story, but will love to listen to the sound of your voice. Now is the time to introduce the first cloth and board books, if you have not done so already.

Hallowe'en is a modern remnant of an ancient fire festival. Why not celebrate with a pumpkin, bonfire, and fireworks? Held in your arms, babe is unlikely to be scared. Let him have his first experience of this exciting time. As long as you are enjoying it, chances are it will stimulate his sense of adventure.

☆ FALL THEMES ☆

- *Count your blessings*
- *Create special mementoes such as a photograph album*
- *Make sure your Baby Book is up to date*
- *Write a diary of memorable baby events, dreams, feelings, and so on*
- *Gather fruit—you can do this with baby, let him smell the hedgerows and feel the slight edge the wind carries*
- *Touch leaves—pick them from the trees if you can to make sure they are clean enough for baby's fingers to scrunch up*
- *Visit ancient monuments with your new baby—to celebrate how the cycle of life renews itself*
- *If you are weaning baby, stew local organic apples and other fruit and freeze some for the Winter*

☆ SIMPLE FALL CHARM ☆

As a simple charm you may like to make your own corn dolly from red ribbon and stalks of wheat. Corn dollies are symbolic of the life that continues from season to season, the wheat of one year being the seeds of the next. If you can, take your babe into a wheat field at the end of summer and pick three stalks. Let your baby listen to the whispers of the wheat as you stand in the golden field. When you have time to sit quietly, bind up the three stalks with red ribbon saying, "Healthy, wealthy, and wise." Imagine those gifts as you do so. This is a charm for your baby, and the dry wheat will keep for a long time—certainly until next year, when you can make another. If you want to be more creative, you might like to experiment with more complex interweavings of golden corn and red ribbon— the colors of life.

BLESSINGS FROM YOUR ANCESTORS

The Celts especially honored the ancestors as Hallowe'en approached. Connect your baby with his ancestors with this simple spell.

YOU WILL NEED:

A purple candle

Lavender or jasmine oil

An oil burner

A photograph of your baby

A photograph of one of your baby's ancestors who has already died

Purple ribbon

Patchouli oil

Light the purple candle, heat the lavender or jasmine oil in an oil burner, and think about your and your baby's ancestors, what they might have been like, how they felt, and what life was like for them. Ask them to give love, protection, and guidance to your baby.

Roll up the photograph of your babe inside that of the ancestor. Cut the ribbon to about 20 inches (50 cm) in length and put a drop of patchouli oil on each end to seal the matter. Tie the photos in a scroll and secure with the ribbon. Your babe is now held in the embrace of the Wise Ones.

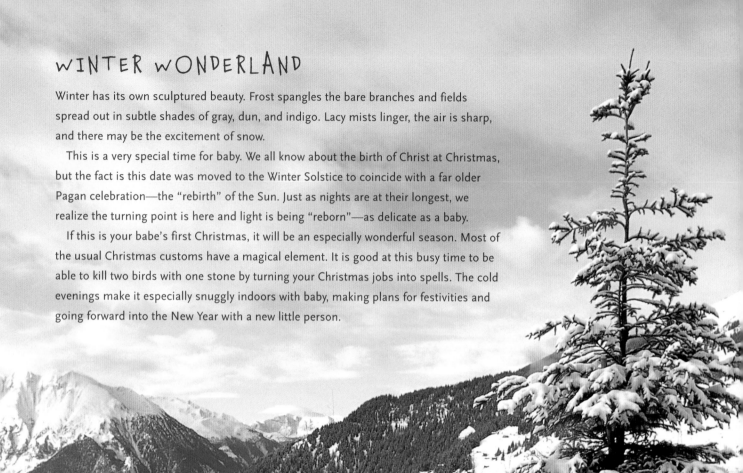

WINTER WONDERLAND

Winter has its own sculptured beauty. Frost spangles the bare branches and fields spread out in subtle shades of gray, dun, and indigo. Lacy mists linger, the air is sharp, and there may be the excitement of snow.

This is a very special time for baby. We all know about the birth of Christ at Christmas, but the fact is this date was moved to the Winter Solstice to coincide with a far older Pagan celebration—the "rebirth" of the Sun. Just as nights are at their longest, we realize the turning point is here and light is being "reborn"—as delicate as a baby.

If this is your babe's first Christmas, it will be an especially wonderful season. Most of the usual Christmas customs have a magical element. It is good at this busy time to be able to kill two birds with one stone by turning your Christmas jobs into spells. The cold evenings make it especially snuggly indoors with baby, making plans for festivities and going forward into the New Year with a new little person.

☆ BABY WINTER THEMES ☆

- *Choose gifts*
- *Send cards as a family—press baby's foot on an ink pad and send her footprint to close friends and family*
- *Sing carols with baby*
- *Let baby experience the winter by touching snow and frost. Don't worry about baby getting cold. Keep her close to you and you will be aware how she is feeling*
- *Make New Year plans*
- *Get your friends together in the New Year to talk about birth experiences*
- *Watch the first bulbs break the frosty ground—let baby touch them*
- *Make New Year resolutions about things you will do with baby*
- *Write a poem about your feelings*
- *Have a party*

MAGICAL CHRISTMAS TREE

Although the tradition of a Christmas tree arrived in the U.S. from Germany in the 1800s, it echoes much older themes. The entire idea of the tree is magical, for the evergreen is sacred to the ever-present Goddess. The tree is an important symbol in old shamanic traditions and the Jewish Kabbalah. When we decorate our tree, we are affirming that life goes on, and many things we hang on it are symbolic. Make a happiness spell out of decorating your tree.

YOU WILL NEED:

Your favorite music

A cinnamon-scented candle

Decorations for your tree

A glass of mulled wine

Put your tree in place. Play your favorite music, light a cinnamon-scented candle, and hold baby. She will want to touch the glittering decorations, so make sure there are safe objects for her to chew and touch. Hang them on the tree, honoring their meanings:

STAR • may the magic of Christmas always be with us

MOON • may we always feel attuned to the cycles of life

SANTA CLAUS • may we recognize and treasure our gifts

BALL • may we always enjoy the sweet fruits of life

SUN • may our lives blossom as the sun returns

TINSEL • may we always be lighthearted

TREE-TOP ANGEL • (she is a Goddess symbol)

we honor and thank you, Great Mother

Make up your own words for any other symbols and finish your ceremony with a warming glass of mulled wine.

bright NEW yEAR

It is exciting to be greeting the New Year with your baby. Continue through January and into the beginning of February, which was and is a time to celebrate creativity of all kinds, because it was the feast of the Celtic Goddess, Bride. As Lady of the Sacred Flame, her gifts are fertility, healing, and all forms of craft. The old tradition of making a "Bridie Doll" as a fertility symbol has been adapted by some modern women to make a festival of all things womanly, especially childbirth. You, too, can make this a time of feminine celebration.

Find a doll that you like—this may be an old one of yours, your baby's, or a new acquisition. Dress her in white, if you like. Invite a group of close and trusted friends and light white candles around the room. Mothers can bring their babies and hold them. Sit in a circle and pass the Bridie Doll around. The person with the doll has her turn to tell the group about her experiences of motherhood or any other feminine experience, happy or sad. The other women listen and give support and understanding. Pass the doll around several times if you like. If your birthing and mothering experiences have been a challenge, this can be soothing. If they have been great, then you are celebrating.

When you have finished, put the dolly on the table and share a white meal—such as cheese, white wine, white grapes, and anything "white" that you like—to celebrate the newness of the year and the cleansing feeling you get from talking about your emotions. Older babes can have a taste of the goodies, too.

☆ EARLY FEBRUARY THEMES ☆
- *New Year's resolutions—which are much easier to make and keep as the light grows*
- *Fresh activities with baby such as walks and more active games*
- *Creativity—why not start a scrapbook of baby memories, write a poem, paint a picture*
- *Sing a song or nursery rhyme to baby*
- *Sew or knit baby clothes, especially in white*

FRESH NEW YEAR SPELL

At New Year most of us feel too sluggish for any real "newness." You can do this spell at any time before the end of February.

YOU WILL NEED:

White flowers in a pot

A white candle

Lavender oil

An oil burner

Two lemons

A white cloth

Pins with colored heads (not black ones)

White ribbon

Put the flowers on the nursery windowsill along with the lit candle. Heat the oil and make sure the lavender fragrance is rising. Cut one of the lemons and squeeze some juice onto the white cloth. Wipe just a symbolic amount around the paintwork, especially the window, saying,

"Be cleansed and pure
New life comes sure."

Sitting comfortably, take up the other lemon and stick the colored pins in it, making a wish for your babe with each one. Red for health and energy, blue for peaceful sleep, yellow for quick learning, orange for happiness and laughter, green for luck, purple for spiritual blessing. Tie the ribbon around the lemon and hang it in the nursery, well away from the crib, making sure it can't fall or be reached by baby.

HAPPY BIRTHDAY!

You can't believe it's been a whole year. But baby is probably saying his first words, taking his first steps—you can see this little bundle is becoming an individual. The first birthday is a magical milestone.

Astrologically, the first birthday is the time of the "solar return". That simply means that the Sun, having made a complete tour of the zodiac, is now back where it was at the time he was born. Every planetary "return" is an intense time, but as adults we have learned how to cope and enjoy it, so we tend only to be sensitive to the slower-moving planets that "return" after many years. Not so baby. If he is extra-excitable or gets upset easily, don't let it spoil your enjoyment of the party. He is just feeling more aware of what it is to be an individual.

Magical birthday party

Baby may not be interested in guests, but have a celebration for yourself, if you wish. Pin some pictures of baby just after his birth on the wall as a reminder of how much he has grown in size and strength. If friends are bringing their tots, take a light and casual approach. Food should be bite-sized pieces of organic sausage, cheese, small crackers and pieces of fruit. Keep a solar theme with bright napkins and gold paper crowns, gold or orange balloons, and a cheerful cake with a candle, of course. When you light the candle, say, "We celebrate the first year of [*Babe's Name*]'s life" and let it burn for a while. Why not change the usual birthday song to:

> *"Happy Birthday to you*
> *I give you love that's true*
> *And wish you happiness, too,*
> *Happy Birthday to you."*

Help baby to blow out the candle—magic candles are more fun because they relight and this will give baby a chance to learn how to blow.

Take a picture of each child with an instant camera and pop it in the party bag with a sprig of rosemary, a piece of cake, a balloon, and perhaps an angel wish card or similar, which you can find in New Age shops. A party to remember.

MAGICAL BIRTHDAY CARD

Here we have a birthday card with a difference. This one you will want to treasure all your life.

YOU WILL NEED:

A large birthday card

A box

Dried rosemary

A white ribbon

Choose a large card and ask all your guests to write a line with a special wish for your baby. After the party place this card in a special box with a little dried rosemary, if you wish. Put any other mementoes in the box, such as photographs and baby's birthstone (see pages 60–67). Tie the box carefully with a white ribbon. When you need a little extra blessing in life, open the box and breathe in the magic.

☆ DECORATING THE ROSEMARY TREE ☆

Rosemary is ruled by the Sun and is for remembrance. It also preserves youth, protects, and brings peace. The rosemary that you bought to welcome your baby will have grown. Bring it indoors, if possible, and decorate it with solar symbols such as gold jewelry, amber, carnelian, tiger's eye, and anything shiny that seems right. Make sure it's out of babe's reach. If the shrub is large enough, cut a small sprig for each birthday guest.

picture credits

Key: a=above, b=below, r=right, l=left, c=center

index

Treloar; **75 inset ph** Pia Tryde; **76a ph** Simon Upton; **76b ph** Debi Treloar; **77 ph** Chris Tubbs; **78 ph** Debi Treloar; **79 ph** Debi Treloar / Sophie Eadie's family home in London; **80b inset & background ph** David Montgomery; **80a insets ph** Dan Duchars; **81, 82, 83b inset ph** Debi Treloar; **83ar ph** Jan Baldwin; **84 ph** Polly Wreford; **85 background ph** Pia Tryde; **85a inset ph** Francesca Yorke; **85b inset ph** Caroline Arber; **86 ph** Debi Treloar; **87a ph** Dan Duchars; **87b ph** Debi Treloar; **88 ph** Lena Ikse-Bergman; **89 inset ph** Debi Treloar; **89 main ph** Polly Wreford; **90, 91 ph** Debi Treloar; **92 ph** David Montgomery; **93 background ph** Alan Williams; **93 inset ph** Lena Ikse-Bergman; **94 ©** Stockbyte; **95 ph** David Montgomery; **96 ph** Debi Treloar; **97 ph** Dan Duchars; **98, 99ar & background ph** Debi Treloar; **99b inset ph** David Montgomery; **100–101 ph** Debi Treloar; **101r ph** David Montgomery; **102 ph** Debi Treloar; **103 ph** Catherine Gratwicke; **104, 105 ph** David Montgomery; **106 ph** Chris Tubbs; **107 ph** Lena Ikse-Bergman; **109 main ph** Caroline Arber; **109 inset ph** Debi Treloar; **110–111 ph** Debi Treloar; **111r background ph** David Montgomery; **112a ph** Catherine Gratwicke; **112b ph** Debi Treloar; **113 inset ph** Polly Wreford; **114–115 background ph** James Merrell; **114 insets, 115r ph** Polly Wreford; **116 ph** Simon Upton; **117 background ph** Jan Baldwin; **117a ph** Debi Treloar; **117b ph** David Loftus; **118–119a & c insets ph** James Merrell; **118–119 background ph** James Merrell; **118b inset ph** Polly Wreford; **119r ph** Polly Wreford; **120 main ph** Simon Upton; **120 inset, 121 ph** Sandra Lane; **122a ph** Polly Wreford; **122b ph** Caroline Arber; **123 background ph** David Montgomery; **123 inset ph** Catherine Gratwicke; **124, 125 background ph** Debi Treloar; **125a inset ph** Polly Wreford; **125b inset ph** David Montgomery.

business credits

MALIN IOVINO DESIGN
t./f. +44 (0)20 7252 3542
m. +44 (0)7956 326122
iovino@btconnect.com
Page 54

BERNARD M. WHARTON
Shope Reno Wharton Associates
18 West Putnam Avenue
Greenwich, CT 06830
t. 203-869-7250
www.shoperenowharton.com
j.hupy@srwol.com
Page 69

acknowledgments

To Daniel, Jonathan, Adam, and Ben, my four
"babies." And to all my friends who have shared
their experiences of motherhood with me.

The publisher would like to thank the adorable little
models: Antonia, Darcey, Florence, Harry, Imani,
Max, Sorcha, and Tobey as well as their parents.